英語訳つき

和食の基本

JAPANESE RECIPES 60

池田書店

はじめに

　繊細で美しく、調理法や盛りつけに芸術的なワザがあり、器や配膳にまで趣向が凝らされた和食は、世界に誇れる日本文化のひとつです。近年は、低カロリーで栄養バランスがいいという健康面もクローズアップされ、海外でも人気になっています。

　この本では、天ぷら、すき焼き、寿司といった海外でも知られている料理から、煮魚、肉じゃが、おひたしといった家庭料理まで、手軽に作れる人気料理を厳選して60点紹介しています。

　勉強や仕事などで海外に滞在するとき、ホームステイ先や家で和食を披露することがあるでしょう。または、外国の方が和食に挑戦したり、日本でも外国人の友人に和食を教えたりと、いろいろなケースがあると思います。いずれの場合も、食を通じてコミュニケーションがとれ、さらに英語や日本語の勉強にもなれば、こんなに楽しいことはありません。

　日ごろ、料理をしない人にも、または初めて和食を作る外国の方にもわかりやすいよう、プロセス写真をふんだんに使って説明しています。ぜひ、和食作りに挑戦してみてください。

Preface

Japanese cuisine is world famous for its delicate beauty, the technical skills required for its preparation and arrangement, even for the pains taken in its tableware and place settings. In recent years it has attracted attention for its healthy balance of low-calorie nutritious ingredients, and is becoming more and more popular abroad.

In this book we will introduce 60 carefully chosen recipes from internationally famous dishes such as *tempura*, *sukiyaki* and *sushi* to home favorites such as simmered fish, *nikujaga*, and *ohitashi*.

When living abroad for business or study, there will be times when you will want to make Japanese dishes at your home stay or apartment. Alternatively, there may be times when visitors to Japan wish to try cooking Japanese style, or to teach Japanese cooking to their foreign friends in Japan. Whatever the situation, there's nothing more enjoyable than communicating over a meal, and studying Japanese or English at the same time.

For readers who rarely cook, or for foreigners who are trying Japanese cooking for the first time, the directions are written clearly and simply with plenty of photos of the cooking process. I hope you have fun cooking Japanese dishes.

日本の行事と伝統食

Japanese Events and Traditional Foods

日本には四季の移ろいとともにいろいろな行事があり、
それに伴う食事を楽しむ習慣があります。

In Japan, there are many events to celebrate the passing of the seasons,
and it is the tradition to eat certain dishes at these events.

おせち
Osechi

正月に食べる祝い膳で、昔は3段重にいろいろな料理を詰めましたが、現代では簡素になってきています。まず、お屠蘇（薬酒または日本酒）で正月を祝い、縁起物といわれる料理を楽しみます。

On the first of January, in the past it was traditional to serve various dishes in a three-tier box, but this has become simplified today. First, a toast to the new year with *otoso* (medicinal drink or Japanese *sake*), and then a meal of dishes considered lucky.

雑煮
Zoni

おせちと一緒に供される餅の入った椀で、正月には必ず餅を食べます。また、鏡餅といって、餅を飾る風習もあります。

Mochi (rice cake) is always eaten at new year, usually in a bowl of soup that is served with the *osechi* dishes. *Mochi* is also used for decoration, as in *kagamimochi*.

七草粥
Nanakusagayu

松の内が明ける1月7日の朝に食べる野草入りのお粥。宴席続きで疲れた胃腸を休める効果もあります。

This rice gruel is eaten to mark the end of the new year celebrations, on the morning of January 7th. After the long holiday season, it is gentle on the stomach.

5

桃の節句
ひな祭り
Momo no Sekku
(Girl's Day)

3月3日の女の子のお祭りには、ひな人形や桃の花を飾って、ちらし寿司や潮汁などで祝います。

March 3rd is girl's day, or the Doll's Festival. It is celebrated with *chirashizushi* and *ushiojiru* (delicately flavored soup), and the house is decorated with dolls and peach flowers.

端午の節句
Tango no Sekku
(Boy's Day)

5月5日の男の子のお祝いには、鎧兜や鯉のぼり、ショウブの花を飾り、ちまきを食べます。ちまきは餅を笹の葉で包んだものです。

May 5th is boy's day, and the house is decorated with *samurai* armor and iris flowers, while carp streamers fly from the roof. The special dish is *chimaki*, pounded rice wrapped in bamboo leaves.

月見
Tsukimi

9月の満月は「仲秋の名月」といって、最も美しい月とされ、酒を飲みながら月を愛でます。月見団子、芋、栗などを盛り、ススキなどの秋の草を飾ります。

The Harvest Moon, the full moon in September, is said to be the most beautiful moon, worthy of praise while drinking *sake* under it. The food for this event is *Tsukimi dango* (moon dumplings), potatoes and chestnuts, decorated with pampas grass and fall wild flowers.

年越しそば
Tosikoshi soba

大晦日（12月31日）の夜に、そばを食べる習わしがあります。「そばのように細く長く生きる」という縁起をかついでいます。

It is traditional to eat *soba* noodles on the last night of the year, December 31st. Like the proverbial *soba*, life should be long.

目 次
CONTENTS

基本の日本食

ご飯を炊き、汁物を添え、主菜と副菜を作る……。
日本食の最もシンプルな献立を中心に、
ごく基本的な料理法を紹介します。

Chapter 1
Basic Japanese Foods

Cook the rice, add a soup, prepare a main dish and some side dishes.
Focusing on simple Japanese menus, the book introduces
the most basic Japanese cooking methods.

日 本 の 朝 食
Japanese Breakfast

あじの塩焼き
Salted grilled
horse mackerel

ほうれん草のおひたし
Marinated spinach

ご飯
Cooked rice

梅干し
Pickled
plum

白菜の浅漬け
Salty pickled
Chinese cabbage

ご飯とみそ汁に、主菜1品、
副菜2〜3品というのが基本。この構成は朝食に限らず、
ふだんの食事の基本でもあります。
魚、大豆製品、野菜、海藻、発酵食品…と、
栄養面からみても、非常にバランスのいい献立です。

**The basic breakfast is rice and *miso* soup,
one main dish and two or three side dishes.
It's not only breakfast — all meals in Japan follow this pattern.
Fish, beans, vegetables, seaweed,
fermented foods... it's an extremely well-balanced,
nutritious menu.**

納豆
Fermented
soy beans

みそ汁
Miso soup

白く炊き上がったご飯は、
日本人にとっての主食です。現代の日本の家庭では、
炊飯器を使って炊くのがふつうですが、ここでは
昔ながらの鍋で炊く方法を紹介します。

米のとぎ方

ポイント－1

最初、米は水分を吸収しやすいので、汚れた水が米に浸透しないよう、1回目はサッとかき混ぜたら、すぐに水を捨てます。

材料（4人分）

米…………2カップ
水…………480cc

作り方

①ボウルに米を入れ、水（分量外）をたっぷり加え、サッと混ぜて、濁った水をすぐに捨てる**A**。
②手のひらを押しつけるようにしながら、かき混ぜてとぐ。水（分量外）を加えてすすぎ、水を捨てる。水が澄むまで、これを3〜4回繰り返す**B**。
③ざるに取って水気をきる**C**。

A

B

C

Piping hot white rice is the staple food of the Japanese.
Rice is usually cooked in a rice cooker in the modern Japanese household,
but here we will introduce the traditional method of cooking rice in a pot.

To wash rice

INGREDIENTS
(4 servings)

1⅔ U.S. cups rice
2 U.S. cups water

DIRECTIONS

① Put the rice in a large bowl, add ample water, stir quickly and discard the whitish water immediately. **A**

② Wash the rice by pressing down on it with the palm of your hand. Add fresh water, rinse the rice and then discard the water.
Repeat this process 3 or 4 times until the water becomes clear. **B**
③ Drain the rice in a sieve. **C**

POINT 1

Dry rice quickly absorbs water. To ensure that the rice does not absorb water from the first rinse, discard the water after the first rinse immediately.

ふたをしたまま炊き上げ、そのまま蒸します。
吹きこぼれそうになったら、火加減を調節しましょう。

米の炊き方

①厚手の鍋に、といだ米と
分量の水を入れ、30分以上
おいて水を含ませる❶。
②ふたをして、強火にかけ
る。沸騰したら、吹きこぼれ

ない程度の中火にして7〜
8分、次に弱火にして約15
分炊く(吹きこぼれそうに
なっても、ふたを取らない)
❷。

③最後に、30秒強火にして
水分を飛ばし、火を止める。
④ふたをしたまま約10分お
いて蒸らす❸。
⑤水で濡らしたしゃもじで

Cook and steam the rice with the lid on.
When it looks as if the pot is going to overflow,
adjust the heat.

How to cook rice

① Place the washed
rice and measured wa-
ter into a heavy pan,
and leave to soak for
30 minutes. ❶
② Cover the pan and
put over high heat.
Bring to the boil, re-

duce the heat to me-
dium to prevent over-
flowing for 7-8 minutes,
and then simmer for
about 15 minutes. (Even
if it looks about to
overflow, do not re-
move the lid.) ❷

③ Finally, turn heat
back to high for 30 se-
conds, evaporate any
excess water and turn
off the heat.
④ Leave the rice to
steam for 10 minutes
with the lid on. ❸

全体をふんわりと混ぜ、蒸気を飛ばす（混ぜないでおいておくと、蒸気が水滴となって、ご飯がふやけてしまうので注意）。

⑤ With a wet spatula, lightly turn over and mix the rice to let the steam escape. (If this is not done, condensation from the lid will drop back into the rice.)

POINT 2

Rice cookers are popular in Japan. They are very convenient - just add washed rice and measured water to the pot and switch it on. The rice cooker has a timer, so you can set the cooker to prepare the rice to suit your meal time.

炊飯器
Rice cooker

*One cup of rice (3 rice bowls) eguals 390 g . When cooked, rice swells to about 2.5 its volume, so use a large pot.

POINT 3

There are two types of rice in Japan: nonglutinous Japonica, used for cooking, and glutinous *mochigome*. Since Japan is a rice country, there are popular brands of rice depending on the type of rice and place of production. Famous brands include *Koshihikari* from Niigata and *Sasanishiki* from Yamagata Prefecture.

Sekihan

赤飯
Red Rice with
Azuki Beans

材料（4人分）

もち米……2カップ
あずき……100g
打ち水
　酒・水……各¼カップ
ごま塩
┌黒ごま……大さじ1
└塩……大さじ3

INGREDIENTS (4 servings)

1⅔ U.S. cups *mochigome* (glutinous rice)
3½ oz *azuki* beans
Uchimizu
┌⅕ U.S. cup *sake*
└⅕ U.S. cup water
Gomashio
┌3 Tbsp black sesame seeds
└3 Tbsp salt

24

結婚式をはじめとする、
さまざまな祝いの席に供されるご飯です。
日本では、赤はおめでたい色なので、
あずきの色をもち米に移して作ります。

下準備

作り方
①あずきは洗って鍋に入れ、水１ℓを加えて強火にかけ、沸騰したら汁を捨てる**Ⓐ**。
②再び水１ℓを加えて強火にかけ、沸騰したら弱火にして約30分、柔らかくなるまでゆでる。あずきとゆで汁とに分ける**Ⓑ**。
③もち米はといで、ざるに取り、水気をきる（Ｐ21参照）。
④②のゆで汁が冷めたら、③のもち米を５時間以上つけて、色を移す**Ⓒ**。

This rice dish is prepared for weddings and other celebrations.
In Japan, red is the color of celebration,
so *azuki* beans are used to color the *mochigome*.

Preparation

DIRECTIONS
① Wash the *azuki* beans, place in a pan, add a liter of water, place over high heat and bring to the boil, then drain.**Ⓐ**
② Add another a liter of fresh water to the pan of beans, put on high heat, bring to the boil then reduce heat and simmer for about 30 minutes until the beans become soft. Separate the beans from the liquid. Strain the beans and reserve beans and liquid in separate pans.**Ⓑ**
③Wash the *mochigome*, drain in a sieve.(See P.21)
④ When the liquid ② is cooled, soak the *mochigome* ③ in it for over 5 hours, to add color to the rice.**Ⓒ**

もち米は炊くのではなく、蒸し器で蒸します。
途中で打ち水をするのが、ふっくら柔らかく仕上げるコツ。

蒸し方

① ざるに網状の布巾（または布巾）を敷き、ゆで汁につけておいたもち米をあける**A**。

② 蒸し器に水を張り、ふたをして強火にかける**B**。

③ 蒸し器から蒸気が上がったら、①を布巾ごと入れる**C**。

④ ふたをし、強火で約40分蒸す。途中で2回ふたを取って、打ち水をふりかける**D**。

⑤ あずきをのせ、ふたをして約5分蒸す**E**。

⑥ 水で濡らしたしゃもじで全体を混ぜ、器に盛って、ごま塩をふる。

Mochigome is not cooked in a pot, but steamed in a steamer.
While steaming, sprinkle the rice with *uchimizu* to puff it up.

How to steam

① Spread a mesh cloth (or a cheesecloth) over a sieve, and add the drained *mochigome*.**A**

② Fill a steamer half full of water, cover with a lid, and bring to the boil over high heat.**B**

③ When ② is steaming, transfer the *mochigome* ① to the steamer with the mesh cloth.**C**

④ Cover again and steam on high for about 40 minutes. While steaming, sprinkle *uchimizu* (sake and water) two times over the *mochigome*.**D**

⑤ Place the beans on top of the rice, cover again and steam for about 5 minutes.**E**

⑥ Use a wet spatula to turn over and lightly mix the *mochigome* and beans together. Serve in bowls, sprinkle with *gomashio*.

ポイント−1

ごま塩は、黒ごまと塩を鍋に入れ、鍋を前後にゆすりながら空炒りします。ごまが、ふっくらしてきたら、でき上がり。

ポイント−2

あずきの代わりに、あずきをひと回り小さくした「ささげ」を使うのも一般的。あずきは皮が破れやすいため、「胴割れ」するといって忌み嫌われる場合もあるからです。

ポイント−3

祝い膳には赤飯のほか、尾頭付きの鯛も欠かせません。丸ごと1尾を焼いた魚は昔から神事や祝いの膳に用いられてきましたが、とくに鯛はめでたいものとされています。

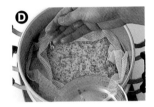

ささげ
Sasage

POINT 1

Gomashio is prepared by slowly heating black sesame and salt in a pan. It's ready when the sesame has puffed up.

POINT 2

Instead of *azuki* beans, it's also popular to use the smaller *sasage* beans. Other beans are preferred because *azuki* beans often split their skins when cooked.

POINT 3

No celebration is complete without *sekihan* and a whole grilled seabream. The tradition of celebrating with a whole grilled fish goes back to old religious rites, and the seabream has long been considered lucky.

栗ご飯
Chestnut Rice

ご飯を炊くときに、いろいろな具や
調味料を加えることがことあります。
なかでも栗を炊き込んだ、栗ご飯は人気の一品。

材 料 （4 人分）

米……2カップ
栗……12個
水……480cc
塩……小さじ1
黒ごま……少々

作り方

①米はといで、ざるに取り、
水気をきる（P21参照）。
②栗は底の部分を切り落と
し、鬼皮をむく。
③渋皮をむいて、4〜6
等分に切る。
④厚手の鍋に①、水、塩、

③を入れ、白米同様に炊
く（P22参照）。
⑤水で濡らしたしゃもじで
全体を混ぜる。器に盛って、
ごまをふる。

**Many other ingredients and flavorings can be cooked with rice.
Among the most popular is rice cooked with chestnuts.**

INGREDIENTS
(4 servings)

1⅔ U.S. cups rice
12 chestnuts
2 U.S. cups water
1 tsp salt
a sprinkle of black
  sesame seeds

DIRECTIONS

① Wash rice and drain
in a sieve. (See P.21)
② Cut off the base of
the chestnuts and peel
the outer hard skin.

③ Peel the inner soft
skin and cut chestnuts into 4 or 6 pieces.
④ Place ① and ③ in a
heavy pan with water
and salt. Begin to
cook in the same way
as white rice. (See P.22)
⑤ Turn over and mix
the chestnuts and rice
lightly with a wet spat-
ula. Serve in bowls,
sprinkle with black

sesame seeds.

豆腐とわかめのみそ汁
Tofu and *Wakame* Miso Soup

みそ汁は、ごく日常的な汁物です。
具にはいろいろな食材が使われ、
それらの組み合わせ方もさまざまです。
豆腐とわかめはポピュラーな具のひとつです。

だしのとり方

材 料（4人分）

昆布……10cm
かつお節……30 g
水……4カップ
豆腐……½丁(150 g)
塩蔵わかめ……40 g
信州みそ……大さじ4

作 り 方

①昆布は濡れ布巾で両面を拭く。鍋に水と昆布を入れ、約20分おく。

②強火にかけて、沸騰直前に昆布を取り出す🅐。

③すぐにかつお節を入れ🅑、弱火で3〜4分煮る。火を止めて、かつお節が沈むまでそのままおく。

④こし器でこす🅒。

Miso soup is a very popular soup.
It can be enhanced with many other ingredients
in many different combinations.
This recipe with *tofu* and *wakame* is one of the most popular.

How to make *dashi* stock

INGREDIENTS
(4 servings)

4 inches *konbu* (kelp)
1 oz *katsuo-bushi*
   (bonito flakes)
3⅓ U.S.cups water
½ block (5¼ oz) *tofu*
1½ oz salty *wakame*
   (seaweed)
4 Tbsp *Shinshu miso*

DIRECTIONS

① Wipe both sides of the *konbu* with a wet cloth. Place water and *konbu* into a pan, and leave for about 20 minutes.

② Place over high heat, remove *konbu* just before it comes to the boil.🅐

③ Add *katsuo-bushi* immediately,🅑 and reduce heat to low for 3 or 4 minutes. Turn off heat; leave it to settle to the bottom of the pan.

④ Drain through a sieve.

🅒

だしをとったら、あとは簡単。
具をサッと煮て、みそを溶き入れればでき上がりです。

みそ汁の作り方

①豆腐は 1 cm角に切る🅐。
②わかめは水につけて戻し、 3 cm長さに切る🅑。
③鍋にだし汁を煮立て、①と②を入れ、沸騰したら弱火にする🅒。

④みそこし器にみそを入れ、だし汁につけながら、へらで混ぜて溶く🅓。みそは煮立たせると香りが飛んでしまうので、煮立つ前に火を止める。

After making the *dashi* stock, the rest is easy.
Add the other ingredients, dissolve the *miso* paste and it's ready.

How to make *miso* soup

① Cut *tofu* into ½-inch cubes.🅐
② Soak *wakame* in water and cut into 1.5-inch square pieces.🅑
③ Bring *dashi* stock to the boil, add ①, ② bring back to the boil then reduce heat to low.🅒
④ Put *miso* into a *miso* sieve, and use a spatula to dissolve the *miso* into the pan of *dashi* stock.🅓 The fragrance of *miso* will evaporate if it is left on the heat, so turn off the heat before boiling.

ポイント-1

昆布とかつお節でとるだし
は日本料理の基本。汁物の
ほか、煮物や和え物など、
ほかの料理にも幅広く使え
ます。多めにとって冷蔵し
ておくと便利。ほかには、
煮干しでとるだしや、昆布
だけでとるだしなどがあり
ます。

ポイント-2

みそには大別して、赤みそ、
信州みそ、白みそがありま
す。赤みそは旨み、白みそ
は甘みが強く、信州みそは
その中間。地方や好みなど
によって使い分けられてい
ますが、みそ汁には信州み
そが一般的です。

ポイント-3

みそ汁の具として一般的な
ものはほかに、油揚げ、長
ねぎ、大根、なめこ、あさ
り、しじみ、豚肉、玉ねぎ、
ほうれん草、じゃがいも、納
豆など、いろいろあります。

白みそ
White *miso*

赤みそ
Red *miso*

POINT 1

Dashi stock made with *konbu* and *katsuo-bushi* is one of the basics of Japanese cooking. This stock is used in a wide range of recipes for soups, stews and salads. It's handy to make a large amount and keep some in the freezer. There are other *dashi* stocks made from dried fish and also from *konbu* only.

POINT 2

There are three main types of *miso*: red, white and *Shinshu*. Red *miso* is flavorful, white *miso* is sweet, and *Shinshu* is in between. People use different *miso* in different ways according to taste and regional preferences, but *Shinshu* is most common for *miso* soup.

POINT 3

Some other popular ingredients for *miso* soup are *abura-age*, leeks, *daikon*, *nameko* mushrooms, clams and small shellfish, pork, onions, spinach, potatoes, *natto*, etc.

信州みそ
Shinshu miso

はまぐりの潮汁
Clam Soup

材 料 （4人分）

はまぐり……8個
昆布……5cm
水……4カップ
酒……小さじ1
薄口しょうゆ……小さじ1
塩……少々
青ねぎ……適量

INGREDIENTS (4 servings)

8 live hard-shell clams
2 inches *konbu* (kelp)
3⅓ U.S. cups water
1 tsp *sake*
1 tsp light soy sauce
salt to taste
scallions to taste

だし汁に薄く味をつけ、具の旨みを味わうのが吸い物です。
みそ汁より高級感があり、祝い膳にもよく用いられます。

作り方

①はまぐりは３％濃度の塩水に２〜３時間つけて、砂を吐かせる。殻と殻をこすりつけて、よく洗う**Ⓐ**。

②昆布は濡れ布巾で両面を拭き、鍋に水とともに入れ、約20分おく。強火にかけ、沸騰直前に昆布を取り出す。

③①のはまぐりを入れ、沸騰したら弱火にし、お玉杓子でアクを取る**Ⓑ**。

④殻が開いたら酒、しょうゆ、塩を加えてひと煮し、火を止め、刻んだ青ねぎを散らす**Ⓒ**。

Dashi stock is light to bring out the flavor of the ingredients. It's a little more luxurious than *miso* soup and is often used for celebrations.

DIRECTIONS

① Soak the clams in salted water (water with 3% salt) for 2 or 3 hours to let them expel any sand. Wash the clams well by rubbing the shells against each other. **Ⓐ**

② With a wet cloth, wipe both sides of the *konbu*, place it in a pan with water and leave for about 20 minutes. Place over high heat and remove the *konbu* just before the water boils.

③ Add the clams ① to the pan, bring back to the boil, reduce the heat to low, and skim the broth with a ladle. **Ⓑ**

④ When the clams open, add salt, *sake* and soysauce, bring to the boil, and turn off the heat. Sprinkle with chopped scallions and serve. **Ⓒ**

Aji no shioyaki

あじの塩焼き
Salted Grilled
Horse Mackerel

焼き魚は、魚の旨みをダイレクトに味わえて、
調理が簡単な人気のメニューです。
あじのほか、鮭、さんま、いわしなどが庶民の味で、
日常の食卓によくのります。

魚の下ごしらえ

材料（4人分）

あじ……4尾
塩……適量
大根……適量
しょうゆ……少々
はじかみ……適宜
防風(P93参照)……適宜

作り方

①あじは、ぜいごを尾のほうから包丁を入れてそぎ取る。反対側も取る**Ⓐ**。
②えらを引き出して、取り除く**Ⓑ**。
③胸びれの下に切り込みを入れ、包丁の先でわたをかき出す**Ⓒ**。
④おなかの中まで水洗いする。

Grilling fish is a very popular and simple cooking method
that allows the flavor of the fish to be appreciated directly.
Salmon, sardine and mackerel pike are also popular,
along with horse mackerel, and are eaten daily everywhere.

Preparation

INGREDIENTS
(4 servings)

4 horse mackerel
salt to taste
daikon (white radish)
  to taste
soy sauce to taste
hajikami (pickled ginger) to taste
bofu (Japanese parsley) (See P.93)
  to taste

DIRECTIONS

① From the tail upward, scrape off the hard scales (*zeigo*) with a knife. Turn the fish over and repeat.**Ⓐ**
② Pull out the gills and cut out.**Ⓑ**
③ Make a slit under the pectoral fin, and scrape out the guts from the belly with the point of a knife.**Ⓒ**
④ Wash the inside of the belly with water.

日本では焼き網や、ガスレンジについているグリルで焼きます。
ロースターやオーブンを利用してもいいでしょう。

魚の焼き方

①あじ全体に塩をふり、そのまま約5分おいて、塩をなじませる**Ⓐ**。
②焼き網を火にかけてよく熱し、①の表側を下にして並べ、強火で焼く**Ⓑ**。

③表側がこんがりと焼けたら裏返し、中火にして中までよく火を通す**Ⓒ**。
④大根は皮をむき**Ⓓ**、おろし金ですりおろす**Ⓔ**。軽く汁を絞る（これを大根おろ

しという）。
⑤③のあじを器に盛り、④を添えてしょうゆをかけ、あれば、はじかみや防風を飾る。

In Japan, most houses have handheld grilling racks or gas-table grills.
Fish can also be grilled in the oven or on an electric grill.

How to grill fish

① Sprinkle salt all over the fish, and leave for 5 minutes to allow the salt to seep into the fish.**Ⓐ**
② Pre-heat the grill well, and place the side of the fish ① that will face up when served. Grill at high heat.**Ⓑ**

③ When the fish is grilled golden brown, turn it over, reduce the heat to medium, and then grill well until the inside of fish is cooked.**Ⓒ**
④ Peel the *daikon***Ⓓ** and grate it with a grater.**Ⓔ** Squeeze out the juice lightly. (This is

called "*daikon-oroshi*.")
⑤ Lay the fish ③ on a plate, put ④ to one side and add a few drops of soy sauce, then garnish with *hajikami* or *bofu* if available.

朝食には下ごしらえのいらない、あじの開き（干したもの）や鮭の切り身（塩をふってあるもの）などもよく用いられます。さんまや鮎のように、わたを除かずに丸ごと焼いて、わたも賞味する魚もあります。

魚は腹側が手前に、頭が左向きになるよう盛りつけます。この状態で上になる側を「表側」、下になる側を「裏側」といいます。

はじかみとは谷中しょうがの甘酢漬けのことで、魚料理のあしらいとしてよく使われます。根しょうがの薄切りを甘酢漬けにした「がり」や、せん切りの酢漬けを赤く染めた「紅しょうが」も仲間で、料理によって使い分けられます。

あじの開き
Dried horse
mackerel

はじかみ
Hajikami

紅しょうが
Beni shouga

がり
Gari

POINT 1

Fish that require no preparation are popular for breakfast: dried horse mackerel, salted salmon, etc. There are also fish that are delicious eaten whole, without removing the guts, such as mackerel pike and *ayu* (Japanese river trout).

POINT 2

Lay the fish on the plate so the head is facing the left and the belly is to the front. In this position, the top is called "omotegawa" and the underside is called the "uragawa."

POINT 3

Hajikami also known as *Yanaka shouga*, is a common accompaniment with fish recipes. It is similar to *gari*, sweet pickled sliced ginger root, and *beni shouga*, red pickled ginger. The various types of ginger are used according to the type of food.

鮭の切り身
Salted salmon

ほうれん草のおひたし
Marinated Spinach

材料（4人分）	INGREDIENTS (4 servings)
ほうれん草…1把（300ｇ）	1 bunch (10 oz) spinach
かつお節……適量	*katsuo-bushi* (bonito flakes) to taste
しょうゆ……少々	soy sauce to taste

野菜をサッとゆで、しょうゆをかけたものが、おひたしです。
小松菜、春菊、せりなどの青菜がよく用いられます。

作り方

①ほうれん草は根元を開いてよく洗う（根元の部分に泥がついていることがある）。

②たっぷりの湯を沸かして塩少々を入れ（塩を入れると色鮮やかにゆで上がる）、

①の根元から入れる**Ⓐ**。

③10秒おいて葉まで入れ、サッとゆでる。

④冷水に取り**Ⓑ**、束ねて根元のほうから手で握るようにして水気を絞る。

⑤3〜4cm長さに切り、ひとかたまりずつギュッと握

って水気を絞る**Ⓒ**。

⑥器に盛って、かつお節をのせ、しょうゆをかける。

Ohitashi is vegetables quickly boiled and served with soy sauce. This cooking method is often used with green vegetables such as *komatsuna*, crown daisy, and Japanese parsley.

DIRECTIONS

① Wash the spinach carefully, especially around the stems. (Sometimes the stems will have soil on them.)

② Bring a pot of water to the boil. Add a pinch of salt (to fix the bright color) and slip the stems ① into the pan. **Ⓐ**

③ After 10 seconds, drop in the leaves and cook quickly.

④ Put the spinach immediately into cold water, **Ⓑ** and bundle the stems and leaves so they face the same direction. Gently squeeze the water from the spinach.

⑤ Cut into 1.5-inch lengths in a log shape. By hand, strongly press

the spinach logs to remove excess water. **Ⓒ**

⑥ Arrange in bowls, sprinkle with *katsuo-bushi* and soy sauce.

Natto

納豆
Fermented Soy Beans

大豆を発酵させた納豆は、朝食によく登場します。
卵を入れるなど、人によって食べ方はいろいろです。

ポ イ ン ト

納豆はにおいが強いので、日本人でも嫌う人がいますが、栄養価の高いヘルシーな食品です。全卵または黄身を入れて混ぜる食べ方も一般的。ご飯にかけずに食べることもあります。

材 料 （4人分）

納豆……3パック（300ｇ）
長ねぎ……5cm
しょうゆ……少々
練り辛子……少々

作り方

①長ねぎは小口切りにする**Ⓐ**。

②納豆を器に移し、糸を引いてネバネバになるまで箸でかき混ぜる**Ⓑ**。

③①、しょうゆ、辛子（だししょうゆや辛子が付いている場合はそれを使っても）を加えてよく混ぜる。

④ご飯にかけて食べる**Ⓒ**。

Natto is often eaten at breakfast.
It can be eaten with rice or
raw eggs according to personal taste.

INGREDIENTS
(4 servings)

3 packs (10 oz) *natto* (fermented soy beans)
3 inches leeks
soy sauce to taste
dash of Japanese mustard

DIRECTIONS

① Chop up the leeks. **Ⓐ**

② Put *natto* in a bowl, and stir well with chopsticks until sticky threads appear. **Ⓑ**

③ Add ①, soy sauce, and mustard (if the *natto* pack includes *dashi* soy sauce and mustard, use that), stir well.

④ Eat with hot rice. **Ⓒ**

POINT

Even some Japanese do not eat *natto* because it has a strong aroma. It is a very healthy, nutritious food however. Most people eat it mixed with a raw egg or raw egg yolk on top of rice. Some even eat it on its own.

白菜の浅漬け
Salty Pickled Chinese Cabbage

漬け物にはいろいろな種類がありますが、
浅漬けは簡単なので、家庭でもよく作られます。
白菜のほか、薄切りにしたきゅうり、なす、大根、かぶなども
同様にして、おいしく漬けられます。

白菜
Chinese cabbage

下準備

材料（4人分）

白菜……⅕個（600 g）
塩……白菜の重さの3%
昆布……5cm×3切れ
赤唐辛子……2本

作り方
①白菜は1枚ずつはがし、芯の厚い部分に包丁で切り目を入れ、大きめのざく切りにする。
②全体に塩をまぶす**Ⓑ**。

③昆布は濡れ布巾で両面を拭く。
④赤唐辛子は一方の端をはさみで切って種を除き、水につけて柔らかくなるまで戻す**Ⓒ**。

There are many types of pickles, but this one is very simple to make
and thus very popular in Japanese homes.
Other vegetables can be prepared in exactly the same way,
e.g., sliced cucumber, eggplant, *daikon* (white radish), and turnip.

Preparation

INGREDIENTS
(4 servings)

⅕ (21 oz) Chinese cabbage
salt (3% of Chinese cabbage's weight)
2 inches × 3 pieces *konbu* (kelp)
2 dried red chili peppers

DIRECTIONS
① Tear off the leaves from the Chinese cabbage one by one, make cuts into the bottom of the stems, and cut into pieces. Ⓐ
② Sprinkle salt all over the Chinese cabbage. Ⓑ

③ Wipe both sides of the *konbu* with a wet cloth.
④ Remove the seeds from the red chili peppers with scissors. Soak them in water until soft.

日本には、小さくて簡便な漬け物器がありますが、
なければ、皿などで重石をして漬けます。

漬け方

①大きめのボウルなどに白
菜を入れ、昆布と赤唐辛子
を散らす**Ⓐ**。
②平皿など5〜6枚（500
〜600ｇ）を重石代わりに
のせ**Ⓑ**、全体をラップで包

んで3〜4時間から一晩お
く（漬ける時間は好みで調
節する）。
③水気を絞り、食べやすく
切る。

ポイントー1

浅漬けは漬ける時間が短い
ので、昆布や赤唐辛子で風
味をつけるとおいしく仕上
がります。風味づけには、
ゆず、青じそ、しょうが、
みょうがなども用いられます。

ぬかみそ漬け
Ricebran pickling

In Japan there is a handy little pickle-making machine.
If you do not have one, use plates for a weight.

How to make pickles

① Prepare a large bowl
for pickling, place the
Chinese cabbage into
the bowl, and then
spread *konbu* and red
chili peppers on top. **Ⓐ**
② Cover with 5 or 6
plates (about 20 oz) to
apply pressure. **Ⓑ** Wrap
the whole in cling film
and leave for 3 or 4

hours, or over night.
(Adjust the pickling time
according to taste.)
③ Squeeze any excess
water out of the Chinese
cabbage and cut into
bite-size pieces.

POINT   1

The pickling time for
Chinese cabbage is
short, so the *konbu*
and red chili peppers
add a delicious pi-
quancy. You can also
season with *yuzu* cit-
ron, *aojiso*, ginger, *myouga*, etc.

ポイント－2

漬け物には、浅漬け（一夜漬け、即席漬けともいう）、ぬかみそ漬け、甘酢漬けなどがあります。ぬかみそ漬けは浅漬けと同じような素材を用い、甘酢漬けはらっきょうやしょうがなどを漬けます。

ポイント－3

梅干しは、梅の実を漬けた酸味と塩味の強い漬け物の一種で、大粒のものと小梅があります。そのまま食卓に出されるほか、おにぎりの具やお弁当などによく用いられます。漬けるのに手間と時間がかかるため、最近では家庭で漬けることが少なくなりました。

らっきょうの甘酢漬け
Pickled shallots

梅干し
Pickled plum

POINT 2

This type of pickling method is also called overnight pickling or instant pickling. There are other types such as ricebran and sweet-and-sour pickling. Ricebran pickling is used for ingredients similar to the above, while sweet-and-sour is used for shallots and ginger.

POINT 3

Umeboshi is a very strong flavored pickled plum made using salt. There are two types with large and small plums. They are eaten as they are with the table and also used as ingredients in *onigiri* riceballs and *bento* lunchboxes. Nowadays they are not usually made at home, because the process is laborious and time consuming.

献 立 の 立 て 方 Creating a Menu

日本食はヘルシーといわれますが、
その秘密は栄養バランスのいい献立にあります。
Japanese cuisine is said to be healthy,
and the secret lies in the nutritious balance of the menu.

　日本には「一汁三菜」という言葉が
あります。これは、ご飯に、汁物（み
そ汁や吸い物）を1品つけ、おかずを
3品つけることで、献立の基本です。

　おかずには、肉類、魚介類、野菜、
豆腐や納豆などの大豆製品、海藻など
がバランスよく配されるよう、また、
焼き物、煮物といった調理法が重なら
ないよう工夫します。

　たとえば…

・ぶりの照り焼き（魚…焼き物）
・肉じゃが（肉・野菜…煮物）
・きゅうりとわかめの酢の物
　　（野菜・海藻…和え物）
といったように組み立てます。

　また、四季がはっきりしている日本
では、その季節の素材を献立に取り入
れるのも「粋」とされます。旬のもの
は栄養価が高いので、栄養面から見て
もこれは理にかなったことです。

There is a saying in Japan: "one soup, three dishes." The basic menu is rice eaten with soup (*miso* soup or consommé) and three side dishes.

The side dishes include a good balance of meat, seafood, vegetable, seaweed, and soy-bean based foods such as *tofu* and *natto*, and are prepared so that no two side dishes are prepared in the same way (e.g., only one grilled or stewed dish per menu). For example:

・Yellowtail *teriyaki* (fish, grilled)
・*Nikujaga* (meat and vegetables, braised)
・Cucumber and *wakame* salad (vegetables and seaweed salad)

Also, as Japan is a country with four seasons, it is thought fashionable to change the menu with the seasons. Ingredients in season are full of nutrition, so it is only natural to try to include them in menus at the right time.

人気の日本食レシピ

ご飯・麺・煮物といったカテゴリー別にレシピを並べました。
家庭料理から、ちょっと贅沢な料理まで、
日本で愛されている人気の料理が勢ぞろいです。

Chapter 2
Popular Japanese Recipes

The recipes are arranged in groups according to rice, noodles,
and cooked meals. All the most popular, best-loved recipes
are here – from home favorites to gourmet dishes.

ご飯もの
Rice Dishes

Onigiri

おにぎり
Rice Ball

材 料（4人分）

ご飯（温かいもの）……
　　茶碗5杯分（640ｇ）
梅干し……8個
のり……2枚
塩……適量

INGREDIENTS (4 servings)

5 bowls (22 oz) hot cooked rice
8 *umeboshi* (pickled plums)
2 sheet *nori* (seaweed)
salt to taste

ご飯を三角や丸形などに握ったもので、
手で持って食べます。
軽食にしたり、お弁当にしたり、
手軽に食べられるので人気。

作り方

①ご飯⅛量を茶碗に入れ、中央をくぼませて梅干し1個を入れる**A**。

②両手に水少々と塩をつけ、左手に①をのせ、梅干しを包むように丸める**B**。

③右手を三角にしてかぶせ、ギュッと握る**C**。

④③のおにぎりを手の上で転がしながら、すべての角をギュッギュッと握る。

⑤形が三角に調ったら、のり¼枚分を巻く。同様にあと7個作る。

Onigiri is a ball of rice in a triangular or round shape to be eaten with the hands. It's popular for snacks and lunchboxes, and convenient for eating outside.

DIRECTIONS

① Put ⅛th of the rice lightly into a rice bowl, make a hollow in the center and insert an *umeboshi*. **A**

② Wet both hands with a little water, sprinkle on a pinch of salt, hold ① in the left hand, cover the *umeboshi* with the rice and shape into a round ball. **B**

③ Form the right palm into a right angle, squeeze the rice in the palms of your hands. **C**

④ While rolling the rice ball in both hands, gently squeeze each side.

⑤ When the rice ball is roughly triangular, wrap

POINT

With their wide variety of fillings— grilled salted salmon, fish roe, *katsuo-bushi* (with soy sauce), tuna and mayonnaise, etc.— *onigiri* are very popular. Instead of plain rice, rice mixed with pickled *takana* or *yukari* is also common.

with a ¼ strip of the *nori*. Make seven other rice balls in the same way.

Sake-chazuke

鮭茶漬け
Salmon and Rice with Green Tea

材料（4人分）

ご飯（温かいもの）
　　……茶碗3杯分（400 g）
塩鮭……2切れ
三つ葉……½把
のり……¼枚
薬味
　練りわさび……少々
緑茶……4カップ

INGREDIENTS (4 servings)

3 bowls (14 oz) hot cooked rice
2 fillets salted salmon
½ bunch *mitsuba* (trefoil)
¼ sheet *nori* (seaweed)
Condiments
　wasabi to taste
3⅓ U.S. cups Japanese green tea

ご飯に具をのせ、お茶をかけたものを、
お茶漬けといいます。
お酒を飲んだあとや夜食など、
軽く食べたいときに向いています。

作り方

① 焼き網を熱して鮭をのせ、両面を焼く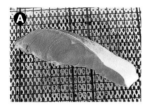。

②①が冷めたら、手で皮と骨を取り、身をほぐす。

③ 三つ葉は細かく刻む。

④ のりは手で小さくちぎる。

⑤ 器にご飯を盛り、②、③、④とわさびをのせ、熱々の緑茶をかける。

ポイント－1

ご飯が冷たいときは、ざるに入れてサッと洗うと、ぬめりが取れて、さらりとした口当たりになります。

ポイント－2

お茶漬けの具には、梅干しもよく用いられます。鯛、うなぎの蒲焼き、天ぷらなど、高級感のある具を使ったものは、料亭などで供されます。

Chazuke is a bowl of rice topped with other ingredients and then covered with Japanese green tea.
It's popular as a late night supper, or after a drink, or whenever a light meal is required.

DIRECTIONS

① Preheat the grill rack, and grill the salmon on both sides.

② When ① has cooled, remove skin and any bones, then roughly flake the salmon with the hands.

③ Cut *mitsuba* finely.

④ Tear the *nori* into small pieces.

⑤ Serve the cooked rice in bowls, place ②, ③, ④ and *wasabi* on the rice, and pour hot Japanese green tea over the top.

POINT 1

When using cold rice, briefly wash it in a strainer to remove any stickiness and keep the rice tasty and fresh.

POINT 2

Umeboshi are also popular as ingredients for *chazuke*. Seabream, eel *kabayaki*, *tempura*, and other delicacies are often served with this dish in classy restaurants.

53

ご飯をサッと煮たもので、「おじや」ともいいます。
鍋料理のあとの残った汁を利用して作ることもよくあります。

材料（4人分）

ご飯……茶碗3杯分
　（400ｇ）
むきえび……8尾
帆立貝柱……8個
三つ葉……1把
だし汁（P31参照）
　……5カップ
酒……大さじ3
しょうゆ……小さじ2
塩……小さじ2

作り方

①えびは背に包丁で切り目を入れ、背わたを取る**A**。
②三つ葉は根を切り落とし、ざく切りにする**B**。
③鍋にだし汁を煮立て、酒、しょうゆ、塩で調味する。ご飯を加えて中火にし**C**、ふたをして約5分煮る。
④①と帆立を入れ、ひと煮立ちしたら火を止め、②を散らす。

ポイント

具には、さまざまな素材が用いられます。ふぐ、かに、牡蠣などの魚介を用いたものは、料亭などで供されることも。家庭で作るときは、鶏肉、卵、にら、きのこなどがよく使われます。

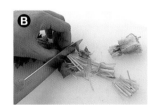

This quickly cooked rice dish is also known as *ojiya*.
It is also common to add rice to the leftover soup from
nabe dishes to make a risotto.

POINT

Many different ingredients are used in this dish. Blowfish, crab and oysters are often served in classy restaurants, while at home it is common to use chicken, egg, leeks, mushrooms, etc.

INGREDIENTS
(4 servings)

3 bowls (14 oz)
　hot cooked rice
8 prawns without
　shells and heads
8 scallops
1 bunch *mitsuba*
　(trefoil)
4 cups *dashi* stock
　(See P.31)
3 Tbsp *sake*
2 tsp soy sauce
2 tsp salt

DIRECTIONS

① Cut the back of the prawn and remove the black vein with the knife. **A**
② Cut the roots off the *mitsuba*, and chop roughly. **B**
③ Pour the *dashi* stock in a pan, then bring to the boil, season with *sake*, soy sauce and salt. Add the cooked rice, reduce heat to medium,**C** cover the pan, and cook for 5 minutes.
④ Add ① and scallops, bring to the boil, turn off the heat, and sprinkle ② on top.

かに炒飯
Fried Rice with Crab

材 料 （4人分）

ご飯……茶碗6杯分（780ｇ）
かに肉（缶詰）……200ｇ
長ねぎ……½本
卵……2個
グリーンピース（缶詰）……½カップ
サラダ油……適量
塩・こしょう……各少々

INGREDIENTS (4 servings)

6 bowls (27 oz) hot cooked rice
7 oz crabmeat (tin)
½ leek
2 eggs
½ U.S. cup green peas (tin)
vegetable oil to taste
salt and pepper to taste

炒飯はご飯を具と一緒に炒めたもので、
元は中国料理です。
具にはハムやえびなどもよく使われます。

作り方

①かに肉は軟骨を取り、手で大きめにほぐす。

②長ねぎは縦に2～3本切り目を入れ、端から粗みじんに切る❶。

③卵は器に溶きほぐす。

④中華鍋（またはフライパン）に油を多めに入れて強火で熱し、③の溶き卵を入れて、半熟状になるまで手早くかき混ぜる❷。

⑤②とご飯を加えて手早く混ぜながら、よく炒める❸（できれば鍋を振り、ご飯にまんべんなく火を通すようにするとよい）。

⑥塩、こしょうで調味し、最後に①とグリーンピースを加えて混ぜる。

Chahan is rice fried with other ingredients,
such as ham or prawns.
It was originally a Chinese dish.

DIRECTIONS

① Remove the cartilage from the crabmeat, then flake roughly with hands.

② Score the leek lengthwise 2 or 3 times, chop roughly from one end. ❶

③ Beat the eggs in a bowl.

④ Pour a generous amount of oil into a wok (or frying pan) and place over high heat, add ③, and stir fry quickly until the eggs are half-cooked. ❷

⑤ Add the cooked rice, and fry well stirring continuously. ❸ (Keep shaking the wok back and forth to cook all the rice thoroughly.)

⑥ Season with salt and pepper, finally add ① and green peas, mix all together.

Nanakusagayu

七草粥
Rice Gruel

普通のご飯より水を多くして炊いたものを、お粥といいます。
七草粥は正月明けの1月7日に健康を願って食べる風習があります。

材料（4人分）

米……1カップ
水……5カップ
大根やかぶの葉……適量
塩……少々

作り方

①米をといで（P21参照）鍋に入れ、分量の水を加え、そのまま30分おく❹。

②ふたをして強火にかけ、沸騰したら弱火にして約30分炊く（吹きこぼれないよう、ふたを少しずらしておくとよい）❺。

③大根やかぶの葉を水洗いして細かく切り、②に加えてサッと火を通す❻。塩で調味する。

七草とは7種の決まった野菜の葉や野草のことですが、現代では、野草は手に入りにくくなりました。そこで正月になると「七草セット」や鉢植えが売り出されます。スーパーなどで普通に買える大根やかぶの葉、せりなどで作るのも一般的です。

Rice gruel or porridge is rice that has been cooked with a little more water than usual.
This version with *nanakusa* is traditionally eaten for good health on January 7th after New Year.

INGREDIENTS
(4 servings)

4/5 U.S. cup rice
4 U.S. cups water
daikon (white radish) or
   turnip leaves
   to taste
salt to taste

DIRECTIONS

① Wash the rice (See P.21), put in a pan, add the measured water, and leave for between 30 minutes. ❹

② Cover the pan, place over high heat, bring to the boil, then reduce heat to low. Cook for about 30 minutes. (Open the lid slightly, so that the water does not overflow.)❺

③ Wash the *daikon* or turnip leaves, cut into small pieces, add ②, and simmer briefly. ❻ Season with salt.

POINT

Nanakusa are seven particular types of herbs, but these are now difficult to find. At new year, you can sometimes find a "*nanakusa* set" in the supermarket, but it is also common to substitute *daikon* or turnip leaves.

七草
Nanakusa

雑煮
Soup with Rice Cake

材料（4人分）

切り餅（角）……4個
鶏もも肉……200 g
大根……1 cm
にんじん……2 cm
三つ葉……適量
ゆずの皮……少々
汁
┌だし汁……4カップ
│酒……大さじ1
│しょうゆ……大さじ1
└塩……小さじ1

INGREDIENTS (4 servings)

4 pieces rice cake
7 oz chicken dark meat
$\frac{1}{2}$ inch *daikon* (white radish)
1 inch carrot
a little *mitsuba* (trefoil)
a little *yuzu* peel
Soup
┌3$\frac{1}{3}$ cups *dashi* stock
│1 Tbsp *sake*
│1 Tbsp soy sauce
└1 tsp salt

丸餅
Rice cakes round
角餅
Rice cakes square

正月の祝い膳に供される、餅をメインにした汁物です。
地方によってさまざまな作り方がありますが、
ここでは関東風を紹介します。

作り方

①焼き網を火にかけて熱し
て餅をのせ、プーッと膨ら
むまで焼く（破裂しないよ
う注意）Ⓐ。

②鶏肉は薄いそぎ切りにす
る。大根とにんじんは薄い
短冊切りにするⒷ。

③三つ葉は根を切り落とし、

ざく切りにする。

④鍋に汁の材料を入れてひ
と煮立ちさせ、②を加える。
煮立ったら弱火にして2〜
3分煮る。

⑤椀に①の餅を入れ、④を
注ぎⒸ、三つ葉とゆずの皮
をのせる。

鏡餅
Decorative
rice cake

Ⓐ

Ⓑ

Ⓒ

This soup with *mochi* rice cake is
traditionally served at new year celebrations.
There are many regional variations,
but this recipe is a Tokyo style one.

POINT

In the *Kansai* region, it
is common to substi-
tute white *miso* for the
soy sauce in the soup,
and to add the rice
cakes whole and un-
grilled. There is anoth-
er tradition called *ka-
gamibiraki* where the
decorative rice cake is
cut and cooked in this
soup on January 11th.

DIRECTIONS

① Pre-heat the grill
well, then toast the rice
cakes on the rack until
toasted and puffed up.
(Be careful that they do
not burst.)Ⓐ

② Cut the chicken into
thin slices. Cut the *daikon* and carrot into thin
rectangles. Ⓑ

③ Cut the roots off the
mitsuba, and chop
roughly.

④ Combine all of the
soup ingredients in a
pan, bring to the boil,
and add ②. When it
comes to the boil
again, reduce the heat
to low for 2 or 3 min-
utes.

⑤ Place ① in bowls,

gently pour in ④,Ⓒ
place *mitsuba* and
yuzu peel on top.

丼 *Donburi*

深い器に盛ったご飯に、おかずをのせたものが「丼」。
庶民的なものから高級料理までいろいろあります。
A deep bowl of rice topped
with another dish is called a "*don*" or "*donburi*."
There are many variations, from home cooking to gourmet versions.

ご飯とおかずが一緒になった丼は、それに汁物や漬け物を添えれば、立派なメニューになるので、手軽に食べられるものとして人気があります。

鶏肉と卵で作る「親子丼」や、牛肉で作る「牛丼」などは庶民的な味わいで、家庭でも簡単に作れます。

とんカツを卵でとじてのせた「カツ丼」や、天ぷらをのせた「天丼」は、作るのにやや手間がかかるので、外食メニューとして人気です。豚肉の質や、天ぷらのネタにこだわった高級なものもあります。

うなぎを甘辛いたれにつけて焼いたものを「うなぎの蒲焼き」といいますが、これをのせたものが「うな丼」です。ただし、伝統を守って作られたうなぎの蒲焼きは高級料理なので、丼ではなく、漆塗りの重箱に詰められ、「うな重」といいます。

A *donburi* meal served with soup and pickles is a delicious menu in itself, which is why it's such a popular meal at home.

The chicken and egg on rice *oya-kodon*, or the beef bowl version *gyudon* are both easy to make and cooked in every Japanese home.

Katsudon, made with pork and egg over rice, or *tendon*, with *tempura* on rice, take more preparation, and are therefore usually eaten at restaurants. There are also gourmet versions of these dishes with high-quality pork cuts or expensive *tempura* ingredients.

Unadon is eel on rice, using eel cooked in the *kabayaki* style, dipped in a sweet hot sauce and grilled. The traditional *kabayaki* style of cooking is a luxury dish, however, and is served in a lacquer box, not a bowl, called *unaju*.

Recently, eel *kabayaki* is available

うな重。粉山椒をふって食べます。
Unaju. Sprinkle a little *sansho* on top and eat.

最近ではスーパーなどで、うなぎの蒲焼きが簡単に手に入るので、それを温めるだけで、家庭でも簡単にうな丼が作れるようになりました。

in supermarkets, and *unadon* is now easily made at home by simply placing the eel *kabayaki* on a rice bowl.

カツ丼
Katsudon

天丼
Tendon

Oyakodon

親子丼
Chicken and Egg on Rice

材料（4人分）	INGREDIENTS (4 servings)
ご飯……茶碗6杯分(780 g)	6 bowls (27 oz) hot cooked rice
鶏もも肉……400 g	14 oz chicken dark meat
長ねぎ……½本	½ leek
三つ葉…… 1 把	1 bunch _mitsuba_ (trefoil)
卵……4個	4 eggs
煮汁	Sauce
だし汁……1½カップ	1¼ U.S. cups _dashi_ stock
みりん……大さじ 3	3 Tbsp _mirin_
しょうゆ……大さじ 3	3 Tbsp soy sauce

家庭でも簡単に作れる丼です。
鶏肉と卵を使うので"親子"の名前がついています。

作り方

① 鶏肉は1.5cm角に切り、長ねぎは斜め薄切りにする。

② 三つ葉は根を切り落として、ざく切りにする。

③ 卵を器に溶きほぐす。

④ 鍋に煮汁の材料を入れて火にかけ、煮立ったら①を入れて中火にする。

⑤ 鶏肉にほぼ火が通ったら、③を回し入れる❹。

⑥ 卵が半熟状に固まったら②を加えて、火を止める❸。

⑦ 丼にご飯を盛り、⑥をのせる❸。

ポイント－1

日本の卵は生食用に作られていますが、外国の卵の場合は火をよく通します。

ポイント－2

日本には丼のサイズに合わせた１人分用の小鍋があります。これで作ると具が丸く、きれいに仕上がります。

A rice-bowl dish that can be cooked easily at home. The name *oyako* (mother and child) is derived from the use of chicken and egg in the dish.

DIRECTIONS

① Cut chicken into ½-inch cubes. Slice the leeks thinly diagonally.

② Cut the roots off *mitsuba*, and chop roughly.

③ Beat the eggs in a bowl.

④ Combine all of the sauce ingredients in a pan, place over high heat and bring to the boil, add ①, reduce heat to medium.

⑤ When the chicken is almost cooked, pour ③ over the top with a circular motion.❹

⑥ When the egg is half-cooked, turn off the heat and add ②.❸

⑦ Put hot rice in bowls, place ⑥ onto the cooked rice.❸

POINT 1

Japanese eggs are produced to be eaten raw, but other eggs should be well cooked.

POINT 2

In Japan, you can find small pans made for single servings. If you use this, the dish will turn out circular and attractive.

Gyudon

牛丼
Beef Bowl

日本には牛丼屋というチェーン店があるほどの人気メニュー。
牛丼屋は日本版ファーストフード店といえます。

材料（4人分）

ご飯茶碗……6杯分（780 g）
牛薄切り肉……400 g
玉ねぎ……1個
煮汁
　だし汁……1カップ
　酒……大さじ4
　みりん……大さじ4
　しょうゆ……大さじ4
薬味
　紅しょうが……適量
　七味唐辛子……少々

作り方

①牛肉は4cm長さに切る。
②玉ねぎは縦半分に切ってから、1cm幅に切る。
③鍋に煮汁の材料を入れて強火にかけ、煮立ったら②を入れる。
④再度煮立ったら①を加えて弱火にし、玉ねぎが柔らかくなるまで煮る。
⑤丼にご飯を盛り、④をのせる。好みで薬味を加える。

This dish is so popular in Japan,
there is even a chain of restaurants called "*Gyudonya.*"
It's a type of Japanese fast food.

INGREDIENTS
(4 servings)

6 bowls (27 oz)
　hot cooked rice
14 oz beef thinly sliced
1 onion
Sauce
　1 U.S. cup *dashi* stock
　4 Tbsp *sake*
　4 Tbsp *mirin*
　4 Tbsp soy sauce
Condiments
　beni shouga to taste
　shichimi togarashi
　　to taste

DIRECTIONS

① Cut the beef into 1.5-inch pieces.
② Cut the onion in half lengthwise, slice into ½-inch pieces.
③ Mix all the sauce ingredients together in a pan, place over high heat, bring to the boil and add ②.
④ Bring to the boil again, add beef, reduce heat to low, and cook until the onion is soft.
⑤ Place hot rice in bowls, place the beef topping ④ onto the cooked rice. Then sprinkle with some condiments, if preferred.

寿 司 *Sushi*

外国でもなじみの深い寿司には、いろいろな種類があり、
外食したり、買ったりすることもよくあります。
Now just as popular abroad, *sushi* comes in many varieties
and is available at restaurants or as take-out.

　寿司の中で一番ポピュラーなのが「に
ぎり寿司」です。にぎったすし飯の上に
新鮮な魚介などをのせたもので、ネタの
種類が多くて華やかさがあり、上質のネ
タを使ったものは高級料理です。おいし
くにぎるにはワザが必要なので、家で作
ることは少なく、寿司屋に食べに行くの
が普通です。

The most popular *sushi* is *nigirizushi*, where fresh raw fish is pressed on a serving of rice. The choice
of toppings is wide and colorful,
and gourmet ingredients can be
added for a luxury meal. There is a
technique to making *nigirizushi*,
and therefore most people go out
to eat it rather than making it at
home.

　にぎり寿司のネタをすし飯にのせたも
のが「ちらし寿司」。新鮮な魚介のほか、
卵焼きや煮た野菜など、いろいろなネタ
を使うこともあります。
　のりですし飯を巻いた「巻き寿司」も
寿司屋の人気メニューのひとつですが、
これは比較的簡単なので、家で作ること
も多いでしょう。

Another version of *sushi* is *chirashizushi*, where the ingredients are
laid on a bed of *sushi* rice. In addition to raw seafood, it is common
to use a variety of ingredients such
as egg roll, boiled vegetables, etc.
Sushi rolls, made by rolling *sushi*
in *nori*, are also popular at *sushi*
bars, and because they are simple
to make, these are also made at

押し寿司の
代表的なものが
「さば寿司」です。
A typical type of
oshizushi is *sabazushi*
(mackerel *sushi*).

にぎり寿司。まぐろ、えび、いか、鯛、いくらなどのネタが一般的。
Nigirizushi. Usually made with tuna, shrimp, squid, seabream, salmon roe, etc.

　ほかに、すし飯に魚介をのせて上から押した「押し寿司」、味をつけた油揚げで包んだ「いなり寿司」などもあります。

home.
Other varieties of *sushi* include *oshizushi*, where fresh seafood is pressed onto rice, and *inarizushi*, *sushi* rice packed inside an envelope of *abura-age* (flavored, deep-fried *tofu*).

いなり寿司
Inarizushi

巻き寿司
Makizushi

Chirashizusi

ちらし寿司
Garnished Sushi

<table>
<tr><td>

材料（4人分）

米・水……各2カップ
昆布……5cm角
合わせ酢
　┌ 米酢……大さじ3
　├ 砂糖……大さじ1
　└ 塩……小さじ1
えび……8尾
焼きあなご……200g
絹さや……8枚
錦糸卵
　┌ 卵……2個
　└ 塩・サラダ油……各少々
しいたけのうま煮
　┌ 干ししいたけ……4個
　├ だし汁……½カップ
　├ 砂糖・みりん……各大さじ1
　└ しょうゆ……大さじ2
しょうゆ・練りわさび……各少々

</td><td>

INGREDIENTS (4 servings)

1⅔ U.S. cups rice, 1⅔ U.S. cups water
2 inches square *konbu* (kelp)
Vinegar sauce
　┌ 3 Tbsp rice vinegar
　├ 1 Tbsp sugar
　└ 1 tsp salt
8 prawns
7 oz broiled sea eel
8 snow peas
Thin omelet (*kinshitamago*)
　┌ 2 eggs
　├ a pinch of salt
　└ a little of vegetable oil
Simmered *shiitake* mushrooms
　┌ 4 dried *shiitake* mushrooms
　├ ½ U.S. cup *dashi* stock
　├ 1 Tbsp sugar, 1 Tbsp *mirin*
　└ 2 Tbsp soy sauce
soy sauce and *wasabi* to taste

</td></tr>
</table>

ひな祭りの祝い膳などとして、よく作られます。
具には刺身用の新鮮な魚介を使います。
好みのものをどうぞ。

すし飯の作り方

作り方

①米をといで、約30分水きりする。鍋に米、水、昆布を入れて炊く（とぎ方、炊き方はＰ21参照）。昆布は沸騰する前に取り出す。

②合わせ酢の材料を鍋に入れて中火にかけて、かき混ぜ **Ⓐ**、砂糖と塩が溶けたら火から下ろして冷ます。

③炊き上がったご飯を盤台（なければバット）に移し、②を回しかける **Ⓑ**。

④水で濡らしたしゃもじで切るように混ぜて水分を飛ばし **Ⓒ**、冷ます。

This dish is often served at the Girl's (Doll's) Festival. Fresh seafood is used for topping. Choose your favorites.

How to make *sushi* rice

DIRECTIONS

① Wash the rice, leave to drain for 30 minutes before cooking. Put the rice, water and *konbu* in a pan and cook. (See P.21) Remove *konbu* just before the water starts to boil.

② Mix all of the vinegar sauce ingredients into a pan, heat to medium, stir until sugar and salt are dissolved, **Ⓐ** and then remove from heat and leave to cool.

③ Transfer cooked rice into a large wooden *sushi* bowl (or vat) and spread ② over entirely. **Ⓑ**

④ Stir *sushi* rice with a wet spatula in a slashing motion to evaporate excess moisture, **Ⓒ** and then cool.

POINT 1

Cook *sushi* rice with less water than regular rice, so that it stays a little firm.

ひとつずつ具を作り、
最後にすし飯の上にきれいに盛りつけます。

ちらし寿司の作り方

①えびは殻をむいて背わた
を取り（P55参照）、ゆで
て半分にスライスする❹。
②あなごはざく切りにする。
絹さやはゆでて、せん切り
にする。

③錦糸卵を作る。卵を溶き
ほぐして塩を加える。フラ
イパンにサラダ油を熱して
卵を流し、表面が乾いたら
裏返す❸。
④裏面をサッと焼いて取り

出し❸、せん切りにする。
⑤しいたけのうま煮を作る。
干ししいたけは水洗いし、
水（または、ぬるま湯）½カ
ップにつけて戻す❹。石突
きを除いて、細切りにする。

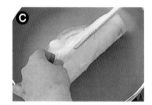

Make the ingredients,
arrange on the *sushi* rice.

How to make garnished *sushi*

① Boil prawns, remove shell and black vein. (See P.55) Cut in half.❹
② Chop the sea eel roughly. Boil snow peas, chop thinly.
③ Make a thin omelet: Beat the eggs and add a pinch of salt. Heat a frying pan with a little vegetable oil, pour in the eggs and spread. When the surface is firm, turn over.❸
④ Cook briefly on the reverse side, ❸ and slice into thin strips.
⑤ Simmer the *shiitake* mushrooms: Wash dried *shiitake* mushrooms and soak them in ½-cup cold or lukewarm water until soft.❹ Remove hard tips , cut thinly.
⑥ Put the *shiitake* mushrooms ⑤ and soaking water into a pan, add *dashi* stock, put over high heat, bring to the boil, then reduce heat

⑥鍋に⑤のしいたけと戻し汁、だし汁を入れて強火にかけ、沸騰したら弱火にして約15分煮る。砂糖、みりん、しょうゆを加え、煮汁が⅓量になるまで煮詰める。

⑦大きめの器にすし飯を盛り、具を彩りよくのせる🄴。好みで、しょうゆやわさびを加えて食べる。

ポイント － 2

干ししいたけは水で戻すと、柔らかくなるのに２時間ぐらいかかります。急ぐときは、ぬるま湯につけると20〜30分で戻ります。

to low and cook for about 15 minutes. Add sugar, *mirin* and soy sauce, and simmer until the liquid is reduced to about $\frac{1}{3}$rd.

⑦ Place the *sushi* rice on a large plate; decorate with the above ingredients (prawn, sea eel, omelet, *shiitake* mushrooms and snow peas). 🄴 Eat with soy sauce and *wasabi* to taste.

POINT 2

Dried *shiitake* mushrooms take about 2 hours to soften in cold water. Soak them in warm water to soften in just 20 or 30 minutes.

干ししいたけ
Dried *shiitake* mushrooms

巻き寿司
Sushi Roll

巻き寿司の中でも、ここでは簡単に作れる細巻きを紹介します。
まぐろを使った「鉄火巻き」と
きゅうりを使った「かっぱ巻き」は細巻きの基本です。

下ごしらえ

材料（4人分）

すし飯……780g
　（米2カップ分）
のり……4枚
まぐろ（さく）……200g
割りじょうゆ
　酒・しょうゆ……各¼カップ
きゅうり……1本
練りわさび・しょうゆ……各適量
しょうがの甘酢漬け…適量

作り方

①割りじょうゆを作る。小鍋に酒を入れて強火にかけ、沸騰させてアルコール分を飛ばす。冷まして、しょうゆと混ぜる。

②まぐろは棒状に4等分に切り、①をからめる。

③きゅうりは1cm各程度の棒状に4本切る。

④のりは、それぞれ半分に切る。

This recipe is for the simple-to-make thin sushi roll. The most common types of thin sushi rolls are tekka maki with tuna and kappa maki with cucumber.

Preparation

INGREDIENTS
(4 servings)

27 oz sushi rice
　(cooked with 1⅔ U.S. cups rice)
4 sheets nori (seaweed)
7 oz tuna loaf
Marinade
　⅕ U.S. cup soy sauce
　⅕ U.S. cup sake
1 cucumber
wasabi to taste
pickled ginger to taste
soy sauce to taste

DIRECTIONS

① Make the marinade: Put the sake into a small pan, bring to the boil over high heat to evaporate alcohol. Cool the sake, and mix with soy sauce.

② Cut tuna into 4 long slices lengthwise, marinate in ①.

③ Cut cucumber into 4 long sticks, about ½ - inch square.

④ Cut nori in half lengthwise.

巻きすを使って一気に巻き、巻きすの上から
形を整えます。コツをつかめば簡単！

巻き方

①巻きす*の目が横になるように広げ、のり½枚を表（ツヤのあるほう）を下にして横長に置く（巻きすの手前のほうに置く）❹。

②すし飯の⅛量（100g）を

①の上に広げる（のりの上部約1cmはあけておく）❸。

③すし飯の中央にわさびをのばし、まぐろを1本のせる❸。

④巻きすごと持ち上げ、中

指で具を押さえながら、ご飯の端と端を合わせるように一気に巻く❹。

⑤巻きすの上から軽く押さえ、形を整える❺。

⑥巻きすをはずし、6等分

Use the *sushi* mat and roll in one movement,
then shape the *sushi* roll by squeezing the mat.
Once you have mastered this technique, it's easy.

How to roll

① Place the *sushi* mat* down so the grain is horizontal, then place the face (shiny side) of ½ *nori* sheet down on it. (Place on the front of the *sushi* mat.)❹

② Spread ⅛th (3½ oz) of the *sushi* rice over ①.

Leave ½-inch at the top uncovered.❸
③ Spread a little *wasabi* across the center of the rice, and lay down 1 slice of tuna.❸
④ Lift the *sushi* mat, hold the ingredients together with the middle

finger, roll up the mat and bring the top and bottom edges of the *nori* together.❹
⑤ Hold the rolled *sushi* mat and squeeze gently to shape the roll.❺
⑥ Remove from the *sushi* mat, cut the *sushi*

に切る。同様に3本作る。
⑦まぐろをきゅうりに代え、
同様に4本作る。
⑧器に盛り、しょうがを添
える。しょうゆをつけて食
べる。

＊巻きすがないときは、2
枚重ねにしたラップで代用
できます。

太巻き
Fat *sushi* rolls

POINT 1

When cutting the *sushi* roll, wipe the knife with a wet cloth after each slice to prevent the rice from sticking to the blade.

roll into 6 portions. Repeat the same process to make another 3 rolls.
⑦ Change the ingredients from tuna to cucumber, and make another 4 rolls in the same way.

⑧ Arrange on serving plates, and garnish with some pickled ginger. Eat with soy sauce for dipping.
*If you don't have a *sushi* mat, use two sheets of cling film to roll the *sushi*.

POINT 2

Sushi rolls using *nori* are also known as *norimaki*. Apart from tuna and cucumber, thin *sushi* rolls are often made with *kampyo*, squid and *natto*. Fat *sushi* rolls contain several ingredients, such as eel, omelet, *kampyo*, *shiitake* mushroom, and cucumber, etc.

いなり寿司
Inarizushi

材料（4人分）

すし飯……780ｇ（米２カップ分）
白ごま……大さじ２
油揚げ……10枚
煮汁
　┌だし汁……1½カップ
　│砂糖……大さじ３
　│みりん……大さじ１
　└しょうゆ……大さじ３
しょうがの甘酢漬け……適量

INGREDIENTS (4 servings)

27 oz *sushi* rice
(cooked with 1⅔ U.S. cups rice)
2 Tbsp white sesame seeds
10 pieces *abura-age*
Sauce
　┌1¼ U.S. cups *dashi* stock
　│3 Tbsp sugar
　│1 Tbsp *mirin*
　└3 Tbsp soy sauce
pickled ginger to taste

78

甘辛く煮た油揚げですし飯を包んだ、魚介を使わない寿司。
お弁当にもよく使われます。

作り方

①油揚げは熱湯で約2分ゆでて油抜きし、ざるに取って水気をきる。

②油揚げを半分に切り、切り口に指を少しずつ入れて開く（静かに開かないと破れるので注意）❶。

③鍋に煮汁の材料を入れて強火にかけ、煮立ったら②を入れ、再び煮立ったら落としぶたをし❷、弱火にして煮る。

④煮汁がほとんどなくなるまで煮たら、火を止めてそのまま冷ます。

⑤④の汁を絞り、白ごまを加えたすし飯をギュッと詰め❸、俵形に整えて油揚げを折りたたむ（油揚げを裏返して作ることもある）。

⑥器に盛って、しょうがの甘酢漬けを添える。

Sushi rice inside *abura-age* (an envelope of sweet-hot flavored, deep-fried *tofu*), *inarizushi* is a type of *sushi* that does not include seafood. It is often used in *bento* lunchboxes.

DIRECTIONS

① Cook the *abura-age* for about 2 minutes in hot water to remove the oil, and drain through a strainer.

② Cut the *abura-age* in two, open the cut edges gently with the fingers. (Be careful not to tear it.)❶

③ Put the sauce ingredients in a pan, put over high heat, when it boils add ②, then bring to the boil again, add a drop-lid ❷ and simmer over low heat.

④ When the sauce has almost disappeared, turn off the heat and leave to cool.

⑤ Press the moisture from ④, and fill the pocket up with *sushi* rice mixed with white sesame seeds.❸ Close up the *abura-age* envelope around the rice, shape it into a roll.(Another version has the *abura-age* turned inside out.)

⑥ Place on plates and add the pickled ginger.

カレーライス
Curry with Rice

材料（4人分）

牛肉……400 g
玉ねぎ……1個
にんじん……⅔本
じゃがいも……1個
塩・こしょう……各少々
サラダ油……適量
カレールウ……1箱
ご飯……600 g
福神漬け・らっきょう漬け
　……各適量

INGREDIENTS (4 servings)

14 oz beef
1 onion
⅔ carrot
1 potato
salt and pepper to taste
vegetable oil to taste
1 block of curry stock
21 oz hot coocked rice
pickles to taste
　(*fukujinzuke, rakkyozuke*)

カレーは、すっかり日本オリジナルの料理となりました。
家庭では、市販のカレールウを使って作るのが普通です。

作り方

①牛肉、玉ねぎ、にんじん、じゃがいもは一口大に切る**Ⓐ**。牛肉に塩、こしょうをふる。

②深鍋にサラダ油を熱して①を炒め、水3カップを加え**Ⓑ**、沸騰したら弱火にし、野菜が柔らかくなるまで約15分煮る。

③火を止めてカレールウを割り入れ**Ⓒ**、かき混ぜて溶かす。その後、弱火で10分煮込む。

④器にご飯を盛って③をかけ、福神漬けとらっきょう漬けを添える。

ポイント
薬味として、野菜を甘辛く漬けた福神漬けや、らっきょう漬け（P47参照）などを添えます。

福神漬け
Sweetly pickled
fukujinzuke

Curry has become a fully Japanese dish. At home,
it is common to make the dish using bought curry stock cubes.

DIRECTIONS

① Cut the beef, onion, carrot, and potato into bite-size pieces.**Ⓐ** Sprinkle salt and pepper on the meat.

② Put the vegetable oil into a deep pan, and add ①, stir fry. Add 2½ U.S. cups of water,**Ⓑ** put the lid on and reduce the heat to low, simmer for 15 minutes until the vegetables are tender.

③ Turn off the heat, crumble the curry stock cube, add it to the stew **Ⓒ** and stir until it is dissolved.Then cook for 10 minutes on low heat.

④ Put the cooked rice on a plate, and pour ③ over the rice. Add the pickles.

POINT

For condiments, add the sweetly pickled *fukujinzuke* and *rakkyozuke*. (See P.47)

カレールウ
Curry stock cubes

Zarusoba

ざるそば
Cold *Soba* Noodles

材料（4人分）

そば(乾麺)……400 g
つけつゆ
  ┌ だし汁……2 カップ
  ├ みりん……¼ カップ
  └ しょうゆ……½ カップ
のり……適量
薬味
  ┌ 長ねぎの小口切り……適量
  └ 練りわさび……少々

INGREDIENTS (4 servings)

14 oz *soba* (dry noodles)
Dipping sauce (*tsuketsuyu*)
  ┌ 1⅔ U.S. cups *dashi* stock
  ├ ⅕ U.S. cup *mirin*
  └ ½ U.S. cup soy sauce
nori to taste
Condiments
  ┌ chopped leeks to taste
  └ *wasabi* to taste

82

そばは、冷たくても温かくても、おいしく食べられます。
シンプルなざるそばは薬味をきかせて、そばの味を楽しみます。

作り方

①つけつゆを作る。鍋にだし汁を入れて強火にかけ、沸騰したら調味料を加え、再度沸騰したら火を止める。冷蔵庫で冷やしておく。
②鍋に湯をたっぷり沸かし、そばを入れ、麺がつかないように箸で軽く混ぜる。
③吹きこぼれそうになったら火を弱め、袋の表示時間ゆでる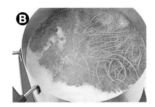。
④ざるに取り、流水で手早く洗い、水気をきる。
⑤器に盛り、はさみで刻んだのりをのせ、①と薬味を添える。つゆに薬味を入れ、そばを適宜つけて食べる。

Soba noodles are delicious eaten hot or cold. This simple *zarusoba* recipe uses condiments to enhance the flavor of the *soba* noodles.

DIRECTIONS

(1) Dipping sauce: Put the *dashi* stock to a pan, place on high heat, bring to the boil, add the other ingredients, boil again and turn off the heat. Chill in the refrigerator.

(2) In a pan, heat plenty of water and add the *soba* noodles. Stir gently with chopsticks to prevent the noodles sticking.

(3) When the pan is about to boil over, turn the heat down and simmer as per the *soba* packet instructions.

(4) Take the noodles in a sieve, rinse the noodles in cold water swiftly, and drain.

(5) Place (4) on plates, cut *nori* with scissors and add, then place (1) and the condiments on the same plate. Add the condiments to the dipping sauce, dip the *soba* noodles in the sauce and eat.

POINT

It's handy if you can find ready-made dipping sauce in a shop. You can also use this dipping sauce for hot *soba* noodles, or for *somen* noodles.

きつねうどん
Kitsune Noodles

材料（4人分）	INGREDIENTS (4 servings)
うどん(乾麺)……400 g	14 oz *udon* (dried noodles)
油揚げ……4枚	4 pieces of *abura-age*
煮汁	Sauce
┌ だし汁……1 カップ	┌ 1 U.S. cup *dashi* stock
└ みりん・しょうゆ……各大さじ1	└ 1 Tbsp *mirin*, 1 Tbsp soy sauce
かけつゆ	Broth (*kaketsuyu*)
┌ だし汁……8 カップ	┌ 6⅔ U.S. cups *dashi* stock
│ 酒……大さじ1	│ 1 Tbsp *sake*
│ みりん・しょうゆ……各大さじ4	│ 4 Tbsp *mirin*, 4 Tbsp soy sauce
└ 塩……小さじ1	└ 1 tsp salt
薬味	Condiments
┌ 長ねぎの小口切り……適量	┌ chopped leeks to taste
└ 七味唐辛子……少々	└ a sprinkle of *shichimi togarashi*

84

うどんとそばは共通のメニューが多く、
きつねそばも人気。名前の由来は、
油揚げがきつねの好物という言い伝えから。

作り方

① 油揚げは油抜きし（P79
参照）、水気をきって、半
分に切る。

② 鍋に煮汁を煮立て、①を
加えて弱火で煮、煮汁がほ
とんどなくなるまで煮て、
そのままおく**A**。

③ かけつゆを作る。鍋にだ
し汁を入れて強火にかけ、
沸騰したら調味料を加え、
再度沸騰したら火を止める。

④ うどんをゆでる（そばと
同様。P83参照）。

⑤ ④をざるに入れ、沸騰し
ている湯につけて温める**B**。

⑥ 器に⑤と②を盛り、熱々
の③をかけて、薬味をのせる**C**。

ポイント

具には、卵、山菜、きのこ、
とろろ（山芋をすりおろした
もの）、かき揚げ、鴨、カレ
ーなど、いろいろなバリエー
ションがあります。

Most recipes for noodles can be used for both *udon* and *soba*,
and *kitsune soba* is also popular. The name *kitsune* (fox) is supposedly
derived from the legend that foxes like *abura-age*.

DIRECTIONS

① Remove the oil from
the *abura-age* (See P.
79), drain the water, and
cut in half.

② Boil the sauce ingre-
dients in a pan, add ①
and put over low heat.
When the sauce is mo-
stly gone, remove from
heat and leave.**A**

③ Make the broth: Pour
the *dashi* stock in a
pan, and bring to the
boil over high heat. Add
the other ingredients,
bring to the boil again,
and take off the heat.

④ Cook the *udon* noo-
dles (in the same meth-
od as *soba* noodles.
See P.83)

⑤ Put ④ in a sieve,
and heat them up by
dipping them in a pan
of hot water.**B**

⑥ Place ⑤ and ② on
bowls, pour on the hot
③, and add the condi-
ments.**C**

POINT

Other toppings for this
dish include egg,
mountain vegetables,
mushrooms, *tororo*
(grated yam), *kakiage*,
duck, curry, etc.

鍋焼きうどん
Nabeyaki udon

Stewed Noodles

材料（4人分）

うどん(乾麺)……400 g
有頭えび……4尾
しいたけ……4個
長ねぎ……½本
三つ葉……1把
厚焼き卵……4切れ（P 106参照）
かまぼこ……8切れ
かけつゆ……8カップ（P 84参照）
薬味
　七味唐辛子……少々

INGREDIENTS (4 servings)

14 oz *udon* (dried noodles)
4 whole prawns
4 *shiitake* mushrooms
½ leek
1 bunch *mitsuba* (trefoil)
4 pieces thick egg roll (See P.106)
8 pieces *kamaboko* (fish cake)
6 ⅔ U.S. cups broth (*kaketsuyu*) (See P.84)
Condiments
　a sprinkle of *shichimi togarashi*

86

コシの強いうどんは、そばと違って煮込んでも美味。
一人用の鍋で煮込み、そのまま食卓へ供します。

作り方
① えびは背わたを取り（P
55参照）、熱湯で赤くなる
までゆでる**Ⓐ**。
② しいたけは石突きを除
き**Ⓑ**、長ねぎは斜め薄切り
に、三つ葉はざく切りにする。
③ うどんをゆでる（そばと

同様。P83参照）。
④ 一人用の鍋に③を入れ、
①、しいたけ、長ねぎ、厚
焼き卵、かまぼこをのせ、
かけつゆを注ぐ**Ⓒ**。
⑤ 強火にかけ、煮立ったら
弱火にし、ふたをして約5
分煮る。

⑥ 三つ葉を入れ、鍋のまま
食卓に供し、七味唐辛子を
ふって食べる。

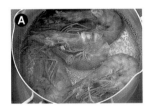  

Unlike *soba* noodles, firm *udon* noodles are also delicious cooked in stews.
Cook them in a small pot, and bring to the table still in the pot.

DIRECTIONS
① Cut out the black vein from the prawns, (See P.55) and cook in hot water until pink.**Ⓐ**
② Cut the hard tips off the *shiitake* mushrooms, **Ⓑ** slice the leek finely diagonally, chop the *mitsuba* roughly.
③ Cook the *udon* noodles. (same as *soba* noodles. See P.83)

④ Put ③ in small pots, add ①, *shiitake* mushrooms, leeks, thick egg roll, place the *kamaboko* on top, and pour on the broth.**Ⓒ**
⑤ Put the heat on high, when it boils, turn down the heat to low, cover with a lid and cook for about 5 minutes.
⑥ Add the *mitsuba*, then bring to the table

with the lid still on. Sprinkle on the *shichimi togarashi* and eat.

そうめん
Thin Noodles

極細麺のそうめんは、うどんの一種。
夏に、ゆでて冷たくして食べるのが一般的です。

材料（4人分）

そうめん(乾麺)……400g
つけつゆ
┌だし汁……2カップ
│しょうゆ……¼カップ
└みりん……大さじ2
薬味
┌長ねぎの小口切り、
│しょうがのすりおろし、
│みょうがのせん切り、
│青じそのせん切り
└……各適量
きゅうりの薄切り……適宜

作り方

①つけつゆを作る（P83参照）**Ⓐ**。
②そうめんをゆでる（そばと同様。P83参照）**Ⓑ**。
③器に冷水と氷を入れ、そうめんを盛り**Ⓒ**、きゅうりを飾る。好みでつゆに薬味を入れ、そうめんをつけて食べる。

ポイント

そうめんより少し太い、冷や麦もあり、そうめんと同様にしてよく食べられます。麺の太さによる食感の違いは、好みの分かれるところです。

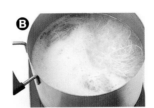

The very thin *somen* is a type of *udon*.
It is commonly eaten in summer: the *somen* is cooked in hot water, then cooled before eating.

INGREDIENTS
(4 servings)

14 oz *somen*
 (dried noodles)
Broth (*kaketsuyu*)
┌1⅔ U.S. cups *dashi* stock
│⅛ U.S. cup soy sauce
└2 Tbsp *mirin*
Condiments
┌chopped leeks to taste
│grated ginger to taste
│sliced *myouga* to taste
└sliced *ao-jiso* to taste
sliced cucumber to taste

DIRECTIONS

① Make the broth. (See P.83)**Ⓐ**
② Cook the *somen*. (same as the *soba* noodles. See P.83)**Ⓑ**
③ Put cold water and ice in bowls, add the *somen* noodles.**Ⓒ** Garnish with cucumber. If you prefer, add the condiments to the broth. Dip the *somen* in the broth and eat.

POINT

Hiyamugi is a little thicker than *somen* but prepared and eaten in the same way. People prefer different noodles according to thickness and firmness.

ソース焼きそば
Sauce yakisoba
Fried Noodles
in Sauce

材料（4人分）

中華麺(蒸し麺)……4玉
豚薄切り肉……200 g
にら……½把
キャベツ……2枚
にんじん……½本
玉ねぎ……½個
サラダ油……適量
ソース
 ┌ ウスターソース……大さじ3
 │ とんかつソース……大さじ3
 └ 塩・こしょう……各少々
薬味
　青のり・紅しょうが……各適量

INGREDIENTS (4 servings)

4 balls of Chinese noodles (steamed)
7 oz thinly sliced pork
½ bunch *nira* (leek)
2 cabbage leaves
½ carrot
½ onion
vegetable oil to taste
Sauce
 ┌ 3 Tbsp Worcester sauce
 │ 3 Tbsp *tonkatsu* sauce
 └ salt and pepper to taste
Condiments
　ao-nori (seaweed) to taste
　beni shouga to taste

焼きそばは中国料理ですが、
ソースで作る焼きそばは日本のオリジナル。
青のりや紅しょうががよく合います。

作り方

① 豚肉とにらは4cm長さに切り、キャベツはざく切り、にんじんはせん切り、玉ねぎは1cm厚さに切る。

② フライパンにサラダ油を熱し、にんじん、玉ねぎ、豚肉、キャベツの順に加え

て炒め、取り出す。

③ フライパンにサラダ油を熱し、中華麺を入れ、水大さじ4をかけてほぐし、炒める。

④ ②の具を戻し、にらを加えて炒め、ソースの材料を混ぜ合わせて加え、サッと

炒める。

⑤ 器に盛り、薬味をのせる。

Yakisoba is a Chinese dish, but *yakisoba* with sauce is a Japanese original. It goes well with *ao-nori* and *beni shouga* .

DIRECTIONS

① Cut the pork and *nira* to 1.5-inch lengths, chop the cabbage roughly, slice the carrots, and cut the onion into ½-inch pieces.

② Pour some vegetable oil into a frying pan, add the carrot, onion, pork, cabbage in order

and stir fry. Remove from heat.

③ Heat some vegetable oil in the frying pan, add the Chinese noodles, pour in 4 Tbsp water and separate the noodles and stir fry .

④ Put ② back in the frying pan, add the *nira* and stir fry. Mix the

sauce ingredients and add, quickly stir fry.

⑤ Put on a plate, sprinkle with *ao-nori* and garnish with *beni shouga*.

刺 身 *Sashimi*

魚介の新鮮さを珍重する刺身は日本の代表的な料理。
家庭でも料亭でも供され、おかずにも酒肴にもなります。
Sashimi, made with freshly caught fish,
is one of the most representative dishes of Japan.
It's popular at home and at restaurants,
and is eaten as a dish or as a snack with drinks.

　刺身は、魚介を一番シンプルに味わう料理です。簡単そうに見えますが、ネタの鮮度や質にこだわることはもちろん、そのネタに合った切り方や盛りつけ方、ツマの種類や添え方などに、いろいろなワザがあります。

　スーパーなどでは、すでに切ったものがツマと一緒になってパックされている

ので、家庭ではそれを購入するのが普通です。生の魚介は冷たくないとおいしさが半減するので、冷蔵庫でよく冷やして食べます。

　しょうゆとわさびで食べるのが一般的ですが、ネタによってはしょうが、にんにく、ポン酢しょうゆなども使います。

Sashimi offers the taste of seafood at its most natural. While it looks simple to make, there are many skills required: an eye for fresh, high-quality fish (of course), the proper way to cut and prepare different seafood, methods and styles for decorative condiments, etc.

In today's Japanese supermarkets, you can find pre-cut *sashimi* with condiments already packaged. These packs are popular to eat at home. The taste of raw seafood is greatly reduced if it's not kept cold, so make sure to keep it in the refrigerator and serve chilled.

Sashimi is usually eaten with soy sauce and *wasabi*, but depending on the seafood, it can also be served with garlic, *shouga* (ginger), *ponzu* sauce, etc.

ツマには、見た目のアクセント、口直し、
殺菌効果などの役目があります。
The condiments are used for visual accents,
as palate cleansers and as preservatives.

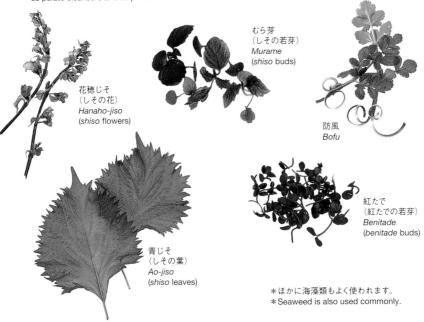

花穂じそ
（しその花）
Hanaho-jiso
(*shiso* flowers)

むら芽
（しその若芽）
Murame
(*shiso* buds)

防風
Bofu

青じそ
（しその葉）
Ao-jiso
(*shiso* leaves)

紅たで
（紅たでの若芽）
Benitade
(*benitade* buds)

＊ほかに海藻類もよく使われます。
＊Seaweed is also used commonly.

奥はまぐろ、左は鯛、右はいか。ツマは、白い糸状の大根のせん切り、青じそ、すだち。
菊の花は飾り。飾り切りのきゅうりにわさびがのっています。
Tuna (back), seabream (left), squid (right).
The condiments are finely sliced *daikon*, *ao-jiso*, *sudachi* (lime).
The chrysanthemum flower is for decoration.
Wasabi is placed on top of the decoratively cut cucumber.

Katsuo no tataki

かつおのたたき
Seared Bonito

かつおは刺身としてもよく食べますが、サッと火であぶった
たたきは、また格別なおいしさがあります。

材料（4人分）

かつおのさく（半身）
……1枚（約600ｇ）
塩……適量
薬味
┌にんにくの薄切り…1片分
│しょうがのせん切り1片分
│青ねぎの小口切り…4本分
│青じそのせん切り…5枚分
└みょうがの薄切り…3個分
ポン酢しょうゆ……適量

作り方

① かつおは金串5本を末広
に刺し、塩をやや多めにふ
って、直火で焼く❹。
② 表面全体が白くなったら
氷水につける❺。
③ 水気を拭き、平造りにす
る（右端から7〜8㎜厚さ
に、包丁を引いて切る）❻。

④ 器に③を盛り、薬味をの
せて、ポン酢しょうゆをか
ける。

かつおのさく
Katsuo fillet

*Katsuo is often eaten as sashimi,
but seared katsuo is also delicious in its own way.*

INGREDIENTS
(4 servings)

1 piece (approx. 21 oz)
  katsuo (bonito) fillet
salt to taste
Condiments
┌ 1 clove sliced garlic
│ 1 piece sliced ginger
│ 4 pieces chopped
│   scallions
│ 5 leaves finely sliced
│   ao-jiso
└ 3 pieces sliced myouga
ponzu sauce to taste

DIRECTIONS

① Skewer the katsuo
on five sticks, sprinkle
with salt, and grill di-
rectly in the flame.❹
② When both sides ha-
ve turned white, dip the
katsuo in ice water. ❺
③ Wipe off the water,
and cut the fillet into ⅓-
inch thick slices pulling
the knife from right
side.❻

POINT

Use uncut katsuo for
this recipe. Keep the
fillets well chilled in
the refrigerator before
grilling, so that even
when seared on the
outside, the inside re-
mains cold and deli-
cious.

④ Place ③ on a plate,
add the condiments,
pour on the ponzu
sauce.

山かけ
Grated Yam and Tuna

すりおろした山芋を、まぐろにかけた料理で、
酒の肴としてもよく供されます。

材料（4人分）

まぐろ……2さく(500g)
長芋……½本
しょうゆ……適量
練りわさび……少々

作り方

①まぐろは1.5cmの角切りにし、しょうゆ少々をかけておく**Ⓐ**。

②長芋は皮をむき、すり鉢でおろす**Ⓑ**。

③器に①を盛って、②をかけ**Ⓒ**、わさびをのせる。しょうゆをかけ、よくかき混ぜて食べる。

山芋は数種類ありますが、長芋が一般的です。すりおろしたものを「とろろ」と呼び、卵黄としょうゆを混ぜて食べたり、ご飯やそばにかけたりします。

This dish features tuna covered with grated *yamaimo*.
It's a popular dish for *sake* drinking.

INGREDIENTS
(4 servings)

2 pieces (18 oz) tuna
½ *nagaimo* (yam)
soy sauce to taste
wasabi to taste

DIRECTIONS

① Cut the tuna into ½-inch blocks, pour on a little soy sauce, and leave.**Ⓐ**

② Peel the *nagaimo*, grate into a shallow tray.**Ⓑ**

③ Put ① in bowls, cover with ②, **Ⓒ** then add the *wasabi*. Pour on some soy sauce, and mix well.

POINT

There are many types of *yamaimo*, but the *nagaimo* is most commonly used. Grated *yamaimo* is called *tororo*, and it is eaten mixed with egg yolk and soy sauce, or poured onto rice or *soba*.

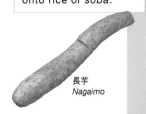

長芋
Nagaimo

Hiyayakko

冷奴
Chilled *Tofu*

豆腐を最もシンプルに味わうのが、
薬味をつけるだけの冷奴で、夏向きの料理です。
冬になると湯豆腐が登場します。

材料（4人分）

絹ごし豆腐……2丁(600ｇ)
薬味
┌長ねぎ……適量
│青じそ……適量
│みょうが……適量
│しょうが……適量
└かつお節……適量
しょうゆ……少々

作り方

①豆腐は4等分して、2個ずつ器に盛る**Ⓐ**。

②長ねぎは小口切りにし、青じそとみょうがはせん切りにする**Ⓑ**。

③しょうがは皮をむいて、おろし金ですりおろし、汁気を軽く絞る**Ⓒ**。

④①に②、③とかつお節をのせる。しょうゆをかけて食べる。

This is the simplest dish using *tofu*: served chilled with condiments, it's ideal for summer. In winter, hot *tofu* is served.

INGREDIENTS
(4 servings)

2 blocks of *kinugoshidofu*
(21 oz)
Condiments
┌leeks to taste
│*ao-jiso* to taste
│*myouga* to taste
│*shouga* to taste
│*katsuo-bushi*
└(bonito flakes) to taste
soy sauce to taste

DIRECTIONS

① Cut the *tofu* into 4 pieces, place two pieces on each plate. **Ⓐ**

② Chop the leeks into small pieces, and cut the *ao-jiso* and *myouga* thinly. **Ⓑ**

③ Peel and grate the ginger, squeeze lightly to remove the excess juice. **Ⓒ**

④ Sprinkle ②, ③ and the *katsuo-bushi* onto ①. Add a dash of soy sauce and eat.

木綿豆腐
Momendofu

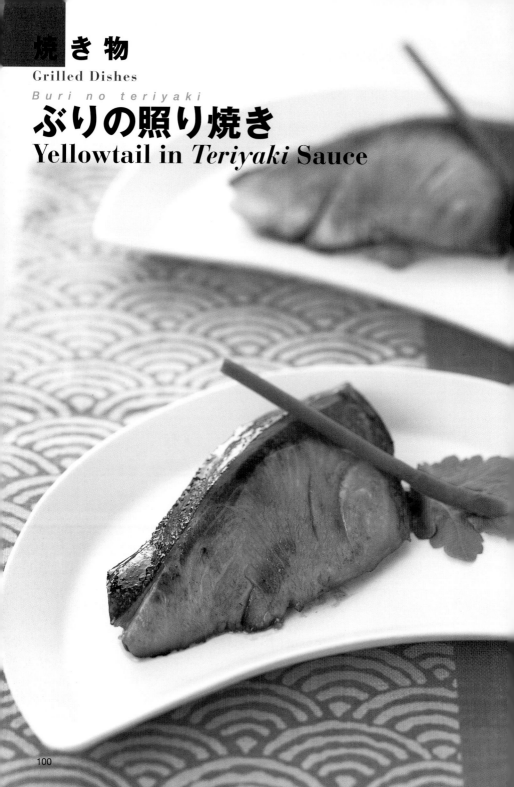

Buri no teriyaki

ぶりの照り焼き
Yellowtail in *Teriyaki* Sauce

照り焼きは、甘辛いタレを素材にからませながら
焼く調理法です。
脂の多いぶりなどの魚に向きます。

材料（4人分）

ぶり……4切れ
たれ
┌ 酒……大さじ2
│ 砂糖……大さじ1
│ みりん……大さじ3
└ しょうゆ……大さじ3
サラダ油……少々
はじかみ（P38参照）
　　……4本

作り方

①バットにぶりを並べ、たれの材料を混ぜ合わせてかけ、ぶりの両面にからめて約15分おく。

②フライパンを熱してサラダ油を薄く引き、①のぶりを並べて入れ、中火で両面をこんがり焼く。

③①のたれを②に加え、ぶりを返しながら両面にからめ、汁をほぼ煮詰める。

④器に盛り、はじかみと、あれば菊の葉などを添える。

Teriyaki is a cooking method
where ingredients are cooked in a sweet-hot sauce.
It's particularly suited to oily fish such as yellowtail.

INGREDIENTS
(4 servings)

4 yellowtail fillets
Teriyaki sauce
┌ 2 Tbsp *sake*
│ 1 Tbsp *sugar*
│ 3 Tbsp *mirin*
└ 3 Tbsp soy sauce
a splash of vegetable oil
4 *hajikami* (pickled ginger)
(See P.38)

DIRECTIONS

① Lay the yellowtail fillets in a shallow baking pan, mix all *teriyaki* sauce ingredients together, pour the sauce over the fish, turn the fish over to coat them, and leave for about 15 minutes.

② Heat the oil in a frying pan, place ① side by side, cook over medium heat until the fillets are golden on both sides.

③ Add the sauce to ②, keep turning the fish to coat them in the sauce, and simmer until most of it has evaporated.

④ Place the fillet onto plates, and garnish with *hajikami* and *kikunoha* (chrysanthemum leaves) if available.

豚のしょうが焼き

Pork Sauté with Ginger

しょうがの風味をきかせた甘辛いたれで豚肉をソテー。
簡単だけどおいしくて、日本ではご飯のおかずの定番です。

材料（4人分）

豚ロース肉……400 g
たれ
┌ しょうが……1片
│ 酒……大さじ2
│ みりん……大さじ1
│ 砂糖……小さじ1
└ しょうゆ……大さじ4
サラダ油……適量
レタス……適量
キャベツ……適量
トマト……適量

作り方

① しょうがは皮をむいて、おろし金ですりおろし、たれの材料と混ぜ合わせておく。

② フライパンにサラダ油を熱し、豚肉を入れ、中火で両面をこんがりと焼く。

③ ①のたれを加え、煮詰めて豚肉にからめる。

④ 器に盛り、レタス、キャベツのせん切り、くし形に切ったトマトを添える。

Sauté the pork with a sweet-hot, ginger-flavored sauce.
This simple but delicious meal is a favorite at dinner time in Japan.

INGREDIENTS
(4 servings)

14 oz pork loin
Ginger sauce
┌ 1 piece ginger
│ 2 Tbsp *sake*
│ 1 Tbsp *mirin*
│ 1 tsp sugar
└ 4 Tbsp soy sauce
vegetable oil to taste
lettuce leaves to taste
cabbage leaves to taste
tomato to taste

DIRECTIONS

① Peel and grate the ginger, then mix it together with the other ginger sauce ingredients in a bowl.

② Heat the vegetable oil in a frying pan, add the pork loin and fry on medium heat until both sides are golden brown.

③ Add ①, and cook until all the liquid evaporates, repeatedly coating the pork with sauce.

④ Place the pork on serving plates, and garnish with lettuce, shredded cabbage and tomato wedges.

焼き鳥
Japanese BBQ Chicken

材　料（4人分）

鶏胸肉……200 g
鶏もも肉……200 g
長ねぎ……½本
たれ
　┌ 酒……½カップ
　│ みりん……½カップ
　│ 砂糖……大さじ２
　└ しょうゆ……½カップ
七味唐辛子……少々
粉山椒……少々

INGREDIENTS (4 servings)

7 oz chicken breasts
7 oz chicken thighs
½ leek
Marinade
　┌ ½ U.S. cup *sake*
　│ ½ U.S. cup *mirin*
　│ 2 Tbsp sugar
　└ ½ U.S. cup soy sauce
shichimi togarashi to taste
sansho to taste

日本には焼き鳥屋があり、お酒を飲みながらつまみます。
たれの代わりに、塩をふって焼くのも人気。

作り方

①たれの材料を小鍋に入れ
て強火にかけ、²⁄₃量まで煮
詰める**Ⓐ**。

②鶏肉は2cm角に切る。長
ねぎは2cm長さに切る。

③竹串に、鶏胸肉を適宜刺
す。鶏もも肉は長ねぎと交
互に刺す**Ⓑ**。

④焼き網を強火にかけて熱
し、③をのせ、①のたれを
刷毛で塗りながら焼く**Ⓒ**。
時々返して、全面をこんが
り焼く。

⑤器に盛り、好みで七味唐
辛子や粉山椒をふる。

In Japan, there are specialist BBQ chicken restaurants
where you can drink while eating grilled chicken.
Instead of sauce, it's also common to sprinkle the skewers with salt.

DIRECTIONS

① Mix all the marinade sauce together in a small pan, bring to the boil over high heat. Reduce until only ²⁄₃rds remain. **Ⓐ**

② Cut the chicken into 1-inch cubes. Cut the leek into 1-inch lengths.

③ Make the *yakitori* skewers: Skewer the pieces of chicken and leek, in alternating order, onto bamboo sticks. **Ⓑ**

④ Preheat a grill rack over high heat, place ③ on top, and frequently brush the skewers with the marinade while grilling. **Ⓒ** Occasionally turn the skewers over, grill all sides until golden brown.

⑤ Place onto plates, sprinkle with *shichimi togarashi* or *sansho* to taste.

厚焼き卵
Rolled Omelet

お弁当や、そばやうどんの具にも
よく使われる卵料理。
ここでは、甘口の関東風を紹介します。

材料 （4人分）

卵……6個
酒……大さじ1
砂糖……大さじ2
塩……少々
サラダ油……適量
青じそ……適量
大根おろし（P38参照）…適量
しょうゆ……少々

作り方

①ボウルに卵を割りほぐ
し、酒、砂糖、塩を加えて
混ぜる❹。

②フライパンを中火で熱し
てサラダ油少々を入れ、①
の¼量程度を流し入れ、全
体に広げる❺。

③卵が半熟状になったら、
向こう側から手前にクルク
ルと巻く❻。

This egg dish is often used in *bento* lunch boxes,
or with *soba* and *udon* noodles.
This recipe is for Tokyo-style, sweet omelet.

INGREDIENTS
(4 servings)

6 eggs
1 Tbsp *sake*
2 Tbsp sugar
a sprinkle of salt
a splash of vegetable oil
ao-jiso to taste
a little grated *daikon*
(white radish)(See P.38)
soy sauce to taste

DIRECTIONS

① Beat eggs in a bowl,
add *sake*, sugar and
salt.❹

② Heat a frying pan
with a little vegetable
oil, pour in about $\frac{1}{4}$th of
① and spread evenly.❺

③ When the egg is half
done, roll egg toward
you from the far end.❻

向こう側から手前へクルクルと巻きます。
これを数回繰り返して、徐々に厚くしていきます。
最後は、巻きすで長方形に形を整えて。

④巻いた卵を向こうへ寄せ、あいた部分を、サラダ油をしみ込ませたキッチンペーパーで拭く。**D**

⑤手前に卵液を流す。**E**

⑥巻いた卵を持ち上げて、その下にも卵液を流す。**F**

⑦半熟状になったら、向こう側から卵を転がして巻く。**G**

⑧④〜⑦をあと2回程度繰り返す。

⑨熱いうちに巻きすにとり、長方形に形を整える

（巻きすがなければ、ラップで代用してもOK）。**H**

⑩食べやすく切り分けて器に盛り、青じそと大根おろしを添え、しょうゆをかける。

 **D**

 **E**

 **F**

Roll the egg toward you from the far end.
Repeat this several times until the egg roll becomes thicker.
Finally, use a *sushi* mat to shape the roll into a long, square block.

④ Push the rolled egg to the far end, and wipe the empty space with oiled kitchen paper.**D**

⑤ Pour another egg mixture into the frying pan.**E**

⑥ Lift the rolled egg, pour the raw egg under the cooked egg.**F**

⑦ When the egg is half cooked, roll from the far end toward you.**G**

⑧ Repeat process ④ to ⑦ about 2 times.

⑨ While hot, wrap the rolled omelet in a *sushi* mat, and press it into a square block. (If you don't have a *sushi* mat, use cling film instead.) **H**

⑩ Cut into bite-size pieces, arrange the rolled omelet on plates, garnish with *ao-jiso* and a small mound of grated *daikon* on the side, and sprinkle with a few drops of soy sauce.

ポイント－1

本来は、卵焼き専用の鍋を使います。これだと鍋が小さいので何回も巻くため、層の厚い、きれいな長方形に仕上がります。

ポイント－2

関西風の厚焼き卵は「だし巻き卵」とも呼ばれるように、だし汁を加え、甘みを抑えてふんわりと焼き上げます。分量は卵6個、だし汁½カップ、みりん大さじ1、薄口しょうゆ大さじ1、塩少々。焼く手順は変わりません。

POINT 1

There is a special frying pan for this dish. Use it to make a thick, perfectly square egg roll.

POINT 2

The Kansai region has its own style called *dashimaki tamago*. Add *dashi* stock to the eggs to reduce the sweetness, and cook until fluffy. The ingredients are 6 eggs, ½ U.S. cup *dashi* stock, 1 Tbsp *mirin*, 1 Tbsp light soy sauce, a pinch of salt. The cooking method is the same.

お好み焼き
Okonomiyaki

Japanese Pancake

材料（4人分）

豚バラ薄切り肉……200g
キャベツ……200g
青ねぎ……4本
紅しょうが……適量
生地
　小麦粉……150g
　水……¾カップ
　長芋……40g
　卵……4個
　塩……小さじ½
青のり……適量
サラダ油……適量
中濃ソース……適量
マヨネーズ……適量

INGREDIENTS (4 servings)

7 oz thinly sliced pork belly
7 oz cabbage
4 pieces scallions
beni shouga to taste
Batter
　5 oz wheat flour
　⅗ U.S. cup water
　1½ oz *nagaimo* (yam)
　4 eggs
　½ tsp salt
ao-nori (seaweed) to taste
vegetable oil to taste
Chuno sauce to taste
mayonnaise to taste

「お好み」という名の通り、魚介や肉、野菜など、
具は何でも好きなものを入れて焼きます。

作り方

①豚肉は 5 cm長さに切り、キャベツと青ねぎは粗みじん切りにする。

②長芋は皮をむき、おろし金ですりおろす。

③ボウルに卵を溶きほぐし、②と生地の材料を混ぜ合わせる。

④③に①と紅しょうがを加えて混ぜる **A**。

⑤フライパンにサラダ油を熱し、④を入れて丸く形作り、中火で約3分焼く **B**。

⑥裏面がこんがり焼けたら返して **C**、約3分焼き、弱火にし、表に返して約3分、裏返して約3分焼く。

⑦青のりをふり、中濃ソースを塗って、マヨネーズを絞る。

Just as the name *"okonomi"* (favorite) suggests,
you can include all your favorite ingredients
in this pancake – seafood, meat, vegetables, etc.

DIRECTIONS

① Cut the pork into 2-inch lengths, chop the cabbage and the scallions roughly.

② Peel and grate the *nagaimo*.

③ Beat the eggs in a bowl, mix with ② and all of the batter ingredients.

④ Put ③ into ①, add *beni shouga* and mix well. **A**

⑤ Heat a frying pan with vegetable oil, pour in ④ with a circular motion, and cook at medium heat for about 3 minutes. **B**

⑥ When the bottom of the pancake is light brown, turn it over **C** and cook for about 3 minutes. Then reduce heat to low, cook both sides for about another 3 minutes each.

⑦ Sprinkle with *ao-nori*, spread with *Chuno* sauce, and garnish with some mayonnaise.

Simmered Dishes
Saba no misoni

さばのみそ煮
Mackerel Simmered in *Miso*

材料（4人分）

さば(半身)……2枚
しょうが……2片
煮汁
 ┌ 水……1カップ
 │ 酒……大さじ3
 │ 砂糖……大さじ2
 └ 信州みそ……大さじ5

INGREDIENTS (4 servings)

2 mackerel fillets
2 pieces ginger
Sauce
 ┌ 1 U.S. cup water
 │ 3 Tbsp *sake*
 │ 2 Tbsp sugar
 └ 5 Tbsp *shinshu miso*

栄養価の高い青魚をみそで煮込んだヘルシー料理。
青魚は臭みがあるので、しょうがを加えて煮ます。

作り方
①さばは半分に切り、皮に
切り目を入れる（味が染み
こみやすくなる）Ⓐ。
②しょうがは皮をむき、半
量は薄切りに、残りはごく
細いせん切りにする。

③鍋に水、酒、砂糖、しょ
うがの薄切りを入れて強火
にかけ、煮立ったら、①の
皮を上にして重ならないよ
うに並べ入れるⒷ。
④水で濡らした落としぶた
をし（P125参照）、沸騰した

ら中火にして5〜6分煮る。
⑤みそを溶き入れⒸ、さら
に約10分煮る。
⑥器にさばを盛り、煮汁を
かけ、針しょうが（しょう
がのせん切り）をあしらう。

This healthy dish simmers nutritious silver fish in miso.
Silver fish have a strong flavor, so ginger is used to counter it.

DIRECTIONS
① Cut the mackerel in half, and score an incision on the skin of each piece (to allow the flavors to infuse the fish).Ⓐ
② Peel the ginger. Slice half of it thinly, and cut the rest into very fine strips.
③ Put water, *sake*, sugar and sliced ginger into a pan, place over high heat. When it has boiled, add ① with the skin facing up, side by side in the pan.Ⓑ
④ Place over high heat, cover with a drop-lid. (See P.125) When it comes to the boil again, reduce heat to medium and cook for 5 or 6 minutes.
⑤ Add the *miso* to the sauce,Ⓒ and cook for another 10 minutes.
⑥ Place the mackerel on a plate, pour the sauce over them and garnish with ginger strips on top.

かれいの煮つけ
Simmered Flounder

114

白身魚は、しょうゆ味でさっぱり煮るのがよく合います。
煮崩れに注意して、きれいに仕上げましょう。

材料（4人分）

かれい……小4尾
煮汁
　水……1カップ
　酒……1カップ
　砂糖……大さじ3
　みりん……大さじ4
　しょうゆ……大さじ4
小松菜……½把

作り方

①かれいは包丁でうろこを
かき取り、裏側に切り込み
を入れてわたを除く❹。
②水洗いし、表側に切り目
を入れる（味が染みこみや
すくなる）❺。
③浅鍋に煮汁の材料を入れ
て強火にかけ、煮立ったら、

かれいを皮を上にして入れ
る❻。
④水で濡らした落としぶた
をし（P125参照）、再び煮立
ったら中火にして約10分煮
る。
⑤器に盛って、煮汁をかけ
る。小松菜をおひたしにし
て（P41参照）添える。

White-meat fish are delicious when cooked with soy sauce.
Be careful not to break up the flesh when cooking.

INGREDIENTS
(4 servings)

4 small flounders
Sauce
　1 U.S. cup water
　1 U.S. cup *sake*
　3 Tbsp sugar
　4 Tbsp *mirin*
　4 Tbsp soy sauce
½ bunch
　mustard spinach

DIRECTIONS

① Scrape the scales off both sides of the flounder, make a slit on the reverse side then scrape out the guts. ❹

② Wash the flounder in water, and score the skin (to allow the flavors to infuse the fish). ❺

③ Combine all the sauce ingredients in a shallow pan at high heat. When it boils, add the flounders with the skin side facing up. ❻

④ Cover with a drop-lid, (See P.125) bring to the boil and cook on medium heat for about 10 minutes.

⑤ Transfer the flounders to plates, and pour sauce over. Simmer the mustard spinach, (See P.41) and garnish the fish with it.

肉じゃが
Nikujaga

Braised Meat and Vegetables

材料（4人分）

牛薄切り肉……200ｇ
じゃがいも……大２個（500ｇ）
玉ねぎ……大１個
にんじん……½本
しらたき……½袋
グリーンピース（缶詰）…大さじ２
サラダ油……大さじ２
煮汁
┌ 酒……大さじ２
│ みりん……大さじ１
│ 砂糖……大さじ３
└ しょうゆ……大さじ３

INGREDIENTS (4 servings)

7 oz thinly sliced beef
2 large potatoes (18 oz)
1 large onion
½ carrot
½ pack *shirataki*
2 Tbsp green peas (tin)
2 Tbsp vegetable oil
Sauce
┌ 2 Tbsp *sake*
│ 1 Tbsp *mirin*
│ 3 Tbsp sugar
└ 3 Tbsp soy sauce

じゃがいもは2種類あり、「男爵」を使うと
煮崩れて柔らかく、「メイクイーン」を使うと
しっかりした食感のある仕上がりに。

作り方

① 牛肉は 4 〜 5 ㎝長さに、じゃがいもは 3 ㎝角に切る。にんじんは半月切りにする。
② しらたきは熱湯でサッとゆでて、ざるに取り、水気をきって、ざく切りにする。
③ 鍋にサラダ油を熱し、牛肉としらたきを中火で炒め

る❹。
④ 肉の色が変わったら、じゃがいも、玉ねぎ、にんじんを加えて炒める。全体に油が回ったら、水をひたひたに加えて強火にする❸。
⑤ 沸騰したら中火にしてアクを取る❻。
⑥ 煮汁の材料を加え、時々

混ぜながら、約10分煮る。煮汁がほとんどなくなったらグリーンピースを加える。

 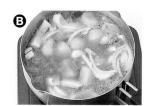 

There are two common types of potatoes.
With Baron type, the potatoes become soft and crumbly.
With May Queen, the potatoes stay firm and crisp.

DIRECTIONS

① Cut beef into about 2-inch lengths, cut potatoes into 1.5-inch cubes, and cut carrot into half-moons.
② Boil the *shirataki* quickly, drain and cut roughly.
③ Heat oil in a pan, add beef and *shirataki*, stir fry on medium heat.❹
④ When the meat chan-

ges color, add the potato, onion, and carrot and stir fry well. When all the ingredients are coated in oil, add water till it barely covers them, and turn the heat back up to high.❸
⑤ Bring to the boil, reduce heat to medium, and skim.❻
⑥ Add all the sauce ingredients, stir occa-

sionally, and cook for about 10 minutes. When most of the liquid has evaporated, add the green peas.

かぼちゃの煮物
Simmered Pumpkin

かぼちゃの甘みを生かすため薄味にし、
弱火でゆっくり煮込んで、ほっくりと仕上げます。

材料（4人分）

西洋かぼちゃ……½個
煮汁
　だし汁……2カップ
　砂糖……大さじ2
　みりん……大さじ2
　しょうゆ……大さじ2

作り方

①かぼちゃはスプーンで種とワタをかき出す。

②くし形に切って、皮をところどころむく（味が染みこみやすくなる。全部むくと煮崩れるので注意）。

③鍋に②を入れ、だし汁を注いで強火にかける。煮立ったら弱火にし、かぼちゃが柔らかくなるまで煮る。

④煮汁の調味料を加えて、さらに10分ほど煮、火から下ろしてそのまましばらくおく。

To preserve the sweetness and crispness of the pumpkin,
this recipe calls for the dish to be cooked slowly with subtle flavoring.

INGREDIENTS
(4 servings)

½ pumpkin
Sauce
　1⅔ U.S. cups *dashi* stock
　2 Tbsp sugar
　2 Tbsp *mirin*
　2 Tbsp soy sauce

DIRECTIONS

① Remove the seeds and fibers of the pumpkin with a spoon.

② Cut the pumpkin into wedges, and peel partially. (To allow the flavor to infuse the pumpkin flesh. Be careful not to peel totally, or the pumpkin meat will fall apart.)

③ Put ② into a pan, add *dashi* stock, and place over high heat. Bring to the boil, reduce heat to low, and cook the pumpkin until soft.

④ Add all of the sauce ingredients, cook for 10 minutes, remove from the heat, and then leave to cool.

筑前煮
Braised Chicken and Vegetables
Chikuzen Style

材料（4人分）

鶏もも肉（骨なし）…200 g
にんじん……1本
しいたけ……4個
ごぼう……1本
れんこん……5 cm（100 g）
こんにゃく……½枚
絹さや……8枚
サラダ油……適量
煮汁
　だし汁……2カップ
　酒・砂糖……各大さじ2
　みりん……大さじ2
　しょうゆ……大さじ4

INGREDIENTS (4 servings)

7 oz boneless chicken thighs
1 carrot
4 *shiitake* mushrooms
1 burdock
2 inches (3½ oz) lotus root
½ block *konnyaku*
8 snow peas
vegetable oil to taste
Sauce
　1⅔ U.S. cups *dashi* stock
　2 Tbsp *sake*
　2 Tbsp sugar
　3 Tbsp *mirin*
　4 Tbsp soy sauce

鶏肉と根菜類やきのこなどを炒め煮にします。
栄養バランスがよくてボリュームもある人気のお惣菜です。

作り方
①鶏肉は3cm角に、にんじんは乱切りに、しいたけは石突きを除いて4等分する。
②ごぼう、れんこんは乱切りにし、それぞれ水に4〜5分さらして、水気をきる。
③こんにゃくは一口大に手でちぎり、熱湯で4〜5分ゆでる**Ⓐ**。
④絹さやはサッとゆでて、斜め半分に切る。
⑤鍋にサラダ油を熱し、中火で鶏肉を炒め、色が変わったら②、③、にんじん、しいたけを加えて炒める。
⑥全体に油が回ったら、だし汁を加えて強火にする。煮立ったら弱火にしてアクを取り、煮汁の調味料を入れ、約15分煮る**Ⓑ**。
⑦煮汁が半分以下になったら強火にし、煮汁がなくなるまで混ぜながら煮、最後に④を加える**Ⓒ**。

This dish is a stew of chicken, root vegetables and mushrooms.
It's filling and well-balanced, and is very popular for dinner.

DIRECTIONS

① Cut the chicken into 1.5-inch cubes, cut carrot into rolling wedges. Cut the stems off the *shiitake* mushrooms and divide it into four equal parts.
② Cut burdock and lotus root into rolling wedges, soak in water for 4 or 5 minutes and then drain.
③ Tear *konnyaku* into bite-size pieces, then boil for 4 or 5 minutes. **Ⓐ**
④ Parboil snow peas, cut in half diagonally.
⑤ Heat oil in a pan, stir fry the chicken at medium fire, and when the meat changes color, add ②, ③, carrots, and *shiitake* mushrooms and stir fry.
⑥ When all the ingredients are coated with oil, add the *dashi* stock, and cook over high heat. Bring to the boil, reduce heat to low and skim, add all of the sauce ingredients and cook for about 15 minutes. **Ⓑ**
⑦ Cook to reduce the liquid to half, turn heat back to high, stir fry until the sauce is almost gone, and then add ④ finally. **Ⓒ**

ひじきの煮物
Simmered *Hijiki*

ひじきは海藻の一種で、とても淡白な味わいです。
油揚げと炒め煮にすることで、コクが出ておいしくなります。

材料（4人分）

ひじき(乾燥品)……30 g
油揚げ……1枚
にんじん……⅓本
サラダ油……大さじ1
煮汁
┌ だし汁……1カップ
│ 砂糖……大さじ2
│ 酒……大さじ2
└ しょうゆ……大さじ3

作り方

①ひじきは水に約20分つけて戻し、ざるに取って水洗いする。

②油揚げは熱湯でサッとゆでて油抜きし、縦半分にして細切りにする。

③にんじんは細切りにする。

④鍋にサラダ油を熱し、にんじん、ひじき、油揚げの順に加え、中火で炒める。

⑤全体に油が回ったら煮汁を加え、中火で汁がなくなるまで煮る。

ひじき
Hijiki

Hijiki is a type of seaweed with a very subtle taste.
It's delicious when simmered with *abura-age* to bring out the flavor.

INGREDIENTS
(4 servings)

1 oz dried *hijiki* (seaweed)
1 *abura-age*
⅓ carrot
1 Tbsp vegetable oil
Sauce
┌ 1 U.S. cup *dashi* stock
│ 2 Tbsp sugar
│ 2 Tbsp *sake*
└ 3 Tbsp soy sauce

DIRECTIONS

① Soak the dried *hijiki* in water for about 20 minutes until soft, pour into a strainer and wash in water.

② Bring the *abura-age* to the boil quickly to remove excess oil. Cut in half lengthwise, and then slice into thin strips.

③ Cut the carrot into thin strips.

④ Heat the vegetable oil in a pan, add the carrot, *hijiki* and *abura-age* in that order, then stir fry at medium heat.

⑤ When all the ingredients are coated in oil, add all the sauce ingredients, and simmer until the liquid is almost gone.

Buri daikon

ぶり大根
Yellowtail with *Daikon*

材料（4人分）

ぶり（切り身）⋯⋯4切れ
大根⋯⋯500 g
しょうが⋯⋯1片
煮汁
┌ 酒⋯⋯大さじ 2
│ 砂糖⋯⋯大さじ 1
│ みりん⋯⋯大さじ 2
└ しょうゆ⋯⋯大さじ 4
すだちの皮⋯⋯適宜

INGREDIENTS (4 servings)

4 fillets of yellowtail
18 oz *daikon* (white radish)
1 piece ginger
Sauce
┌ 2 Tbsp *sake*
│ 1 Tbsp sugar
│ 2 Tbsp *mirin*
└ 4 Tbsp soy sauce
sudachi peel to taste

ぶりも大根も冬が旬なので、寒い季節によく登場する煮物です。
ぶりの代わりに牛肉を使ってもおいしく仕上がります。

作り方
①ぶりは 2 ～ 3 等分に切り、熱湯でサッとゆでてざるに取る❶。
②大根は 3 ～ 4 cm厚さの半月切りにし、鍋に入れて水をかぶるくらいに注ぎ、強火にかける❷。煮立ったら弱火にし、約15分煮て、ざるに取る。
③しょうがは薄切りにする。
④鍋に①、②、③を入れて水をひたひたに注ぎ、強火にかける。煮立ったら弱火にしてアクを取り、煮汁の材料を入れる。
⑤水で濡らした落としぶたをして、煮汁が1/3量になるまで煮る❸。
⑥器に盛り、あれば香りづけに、すだちの皮のせん切りをあしらう。

Both yellowtail and *daikon* are in season in the winter,
so they are often served in simmered dishes.
It's also delicious to substitute beef instead of yellowtail.

DIRECTIONS

① Cut the yellowtail into 2 or 3 equal pieces and quickly cook in boiling water, then drain. ❶

② Cut the *daikon* into 1.5-inch half-moons, put in a pan with water to just cover them, boil on high heat. ❷ When the water boils, lower the heat and cook for about 15 minutes, then drain.

③ Cut the ginger into thin slices.

④ Put ①, ②, and ③ into a pan with just enough water to cover them, cook on high heat. When it boils, reduce heat to low, and skim the surface and then add all the sauce ingredients.

⑤ Place a drop-lid on the surface of the soup and reduce until $\frac{1}{3}$rd the volume.❸

⑥ Serve on a plate, and add the *sudachi* peel for aroma, if available.

揚げ物
Fried Dishes
Tempura

天ぷら
Tempura

材料（4人分）	INGREDIENTS (4 servings)
えび……8尾	8 prawns
いかの胴……1ぱい	1 squid (without the legs)
さつまいも……½本	½ sweet potato
れんこん……½本	½ lotus root
ししとう……8個	8 sweet peppers
衣	*Tempura batter*
┌ 溶き卵1個分＋冷水…1カップ	┌ 1 U.S. cup beaten egg and ice water
└ 小麦粉……1カップ	└ 1 U.S. cup wheat flour
揚げ油……適量	vegetable oil for frying
天つゆ	Dipping sauce (*tentsuyu*)
┌ だし汁……2カップ	┌ 1⅔ U.S. cups *dashi* stock
│ みりん……¼カップ	│ ⅕ U.S. cup *mirin*
└ しょうゆ……¼カップ	└ ⅕ U.S. cup soy sauce
大根おろし（P38参照）……適量	grated *daikon* (white radish)(See P.38) to taste
しょうがのすりおろし……適量	grated ginger to taste

日本料理を代表する揚げ物です。ネタは、季節の魚介や野菜、山菜など、
好みのものをどうぞ。衣を薄くつけ、素材の味が生きるようにサクッと揚げます。

下準備

作り方

①鍋に天つゆの材料を入れて強火にかけ、ひと煮立ちさせ、冷ましておく。

②えびは背わたを取り（P55参照）、尾の先を切り、包丁で尾をしごいて水を出す**A**（水がたまっていると揚げたとき油がはねる）。

③えびの腹に2〜3本切り目を入れる**B**（揚げたとき、えびが曲がらないように）。

④いかは一口大に切り、表面に斜め格子に切り目を入れる**C**（火の通りがよく、食べやすい）。

⑤さつまいもはよく洗い、皮つきのまま5mm厚さの輪切りにする。れんこんは皮をむいて5mm厚さの半月切りにする。

⑥ししとうは縦に切り目を入れる（揚げたとき破裂しないように）。

This deep-fried food is a national dish. Use all your favorite seasonal ingredients – seafood, vegetables and mountain vegetables.
The batter is thin and crispy, to reveal the natural flavor of the ingredients.

Preparation

DIRECTIONS

① Mix all the dipping sauce ingredients together in a pan, bring to the boil, then remove from the heat and cool.

② Remove the black vein from the prawns, (See P.55) cut the tip off the tail, press out any water with a knife. **A**(If water remains in the tail, the oil will spit.)

③ Make 2 or 3 shallow cuts across the belly of the prawns **B** (to prevent curling).

④ Cut the squid into bite-sized pieces, and make shallow, diagonal criss-cross cuts onto the surface. **C** (The notches are important; they make it quick to cook and easy to eat.)

⑤ Wash the sweet potato well, leave the skin on, and cut into $\frac{1}{5}$-inch round pieces. Peel the lotus root, and cut into $\frac{1}{5}$-inch half-moons.

⑥ Score the sweet peppers lengthwise (to prevent them from exploding).

衣には必ず冷水を使い、揚げるときは 一度にたくさん入れないこと。
サクッと揚げるためのコツです。

揚げ物

①衣を作る。ボウルで溶き卵と冷水を混ぜ（必ず冷水を使う）、次に小麦粉を加えて、さっくり混ぜる（混ぜ過ぎない）**Ⓐ**。
②鍋に油をたっぷり入れ、高温（180℃）に熱する。
③えび1尾を取り、衣をく ぐらせ**Ⓑ**、②に入れる。
④同様に少しずつ入れる**Ⓒ**（入れすぎると油の温度が下がるのでよくない）。
⑤1〜2度返して、カリッと揚がったものから、キッチンペーパーを敷いたバットに取り、油をきる（重ね ないように並べていく）**Ⓓ**。
⑥すべての素材を揚げ、器に盛り、天つゆと大根おろし、しょうがを添える。

Two tips to ensure crispy tempura: *Use cold water in the batter,*
and when frying do not put too many items into the oil at the same time.

How to fry

① Make the batter: Beat the egg in a bowl, add ice water (always use ice water) and mix. Add the flour and mix lightly. (Don't mix too well.) **Ⓐ**
② Fill a pan with vegetable oil and heat to high temperature (360°F).
③ Dip a prawn into the batter, **Ⓑ** and slide into ②.
④ Repeat the same process for all ingredients, but only cook a few items at one time. **Ⓒ** (If you put too many ingredients into the oil at the same time, the oil temperature will drop.)
⑤ Turn the items over 1 or 2 times, remove when golden and crispy, and remove excess oil by leaving them on kitchen paper in a tray. (Don't stack them on top of each other,

天丼
Tendon

but lay side by side.)

⑥ Repeat the same
process for all ingredi-
ents, and then arrange
on serving plates, and
serve with dipping
sauce, grated *daikon*
and ginger.

POINT 1

Tempura is also deli-
cious sprinkled with
salt or the *sudachi* (or
lemon) juice instead of
tentsuyu.

POINT 2

Place *tempura* onto hot
rice, pour a little thick
tentsuyu over the top to
make *tendon*. Or add to
cold *soba* noodles for
tenzaru, or hot *soba* for
tempura soba.

かき揚げ
Kakiage

かき揚げ
Kakiage

<table>
<tr><td>

材料（4人分）

むきえび……200 g
小柱*……200 g
三つ葉……1把
衣
┌ 溶き卵1個分＋冷水
│　……1カップ
└ 小麦粉……1カップ
小麦粉……大さじ4
揚げ油……適量
塩……少々
レモン……適量
*小柱…ばかがいの貝柱（なければ、
あさりやいかで代用しても）

</td><td>

INGREDIENTS (4 servings)

7 oz peeled shrimps
7 oz small scallops*
1 bunch *mitsuba* (trefoil)
Batter
┌ 1 U.S. cup beaten egg and ice water
└ 1 U.S. cup flour
4 Tbsp wheat flour
vegetable oil for frying
salt to taste
lemon to taste
*If small scallops are not available,
substitute short-neck clams or squid.

</td></tr>
</table>

細かく刻んだ数種の素材をまとめて揚げます。
天ぷらの一種ですが、天ぷらより手軽で
庶民的な揚げ物です。

作り方

①むきえびと三つ葉は細か
く切り、小柱と合わせる。
②衣を作る（P127参照）。
③揚げ油を高温（180℃）
に熱する。
④①の¼量を小さいボウル
に入れ、小麦粉大さじ1を

まぶす❹。
⑤④に衣大さじ2を加え❺、
さっくりと混ぜる。
⑥⑤をお玉じゃくしに取
り、③に静かに入れる❻。
⑦④〜⑥を3回繰り返し、
2〜3回返してカリッと揚
がったものから、キッチン

ペーパーを敷いたバットに
取って油をきる。
⑧器に盛り、塩とレモンを
添える。

Kakiage is a deep-fried cake of several minced ingredients.
Although it's a type of *tempura*, it is much easier to make and
thus a very popular deep-fried dish.

DIRECTIONS

① Chop the shrimps and
mitsuba finely, and mix
together with the scal-
lops.
② Make the batter. (See
P.127)
③ Fill a pan with veg-
etable oil, heat to high
temperature (360˚F).
④ Put ¼ amount of ①
into a small bowl; dust
with 1 Tbsp of flour.❹

⑤ Add 2Tbsp of batter
into ④ ❺, mix lightly.
⑥ Put ⑤ on a ladle; and
carefully slide it into ③.
❻
⑦ Repeat process ④ to
⑥ several times, turn
the first item over 2 or 3
times until golden and
crispy, then remove and
drain them on kitchen
paper in a tray.
⑧ Place the *kakiage* on

plates with lemon and
salt.

鶏の竜田揚げ
Deep-fried
Marinated Chicken

鶏肉に下味をつけ、片栗粉をつけて、から揚げにします。
フライドチキンよりさっぱりとした香ばしい揚げ物です。

材料（4人分）

鶏もも肉……2枚（400ｇ）
つけ汁
┌ 酒……大さじ3
│ みりん……大さじ2
│ しょうゆ……大さじ3
└ しょうが汁……大さじ1
片栗粉……適量
揚げ油……適量
サラダ菜……適量
レモン……適量

作り方

① 鶏肉は一口大に切る。
② つけ汁の材料を混ぜ合わせ、①を約15分つける 。
③ ②の鶏肉を取り出して片栗粉をまぶし 、余分な粉を払い落とす。
④ 揚げ油を中温（170℃）に熱し、③を少しずつ入れ、途中で返しながらじっくり揚げ 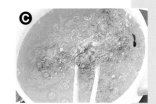、中までよく火を通す。
⑤ キッチンペーパーを敷いたバットに取り、重ねないように並べて油をきる。
⑥ 器に盛り、サラダ菜とレモンを添える。

This dish comprises deep-fried chicken that has been marinated
and dipped in *katakuriko* starch.
It's a tasty, lighter version of regular fried chicken.

INGREDIENTS
(4 servings)

2 pieces (14 oz) chicken thighs
Marinade
┌ 3 Tbsp *sake*
│ 2 Tbsp *mirin*
│ 3 Tbsp soy sauce
└ 1 Tbsp ginger juice
katakuriko starch
vegetable oil for frying
salad leaves to taste
lemon to taste

DIRECTIONS

① Cut the chicken into bite-sized pieces.
② Mix all the marinade ingredients together, add ① and leave to marinade for about 15 minutes. **A**
③ Wipe ②, and dust them with the *katakuriko* starch. **B** *Shake* off extra starch.
④ Heat the vegetable oil to medium temperature (340°F), put a few ③ into the oil, turn them over frequently and fry very well. **C**
⑤ Drain them on kitchen paper in a tray, without stacking them.
⑥ Serve on plates, and garnish with salad leaves and wedges of lemon.

牡蠣フライ
Kaki furai
Deep-fried Oysters

材料（4人分）

牡蠣……20個
塩・こしょう……各少々
衣
　┌小麦粉……適量
　├溶き卵……1個分
　└パン粉……適量
揚げ油……適量
キャベツ……適量
クレソン……適量
レモン……適量
ウスターソース……適量

INGREDIENTS (4 servings)

20 oysters
salt and pepper to taste
Batter
　┌wheat flour
　├1 beaten egg
　└dried breadcrumbs
vegetable oil for frying
cabbage to taste
watercress to taste
lemon to taste
Worcester sauce to taste

フライは西洋料理ですが、牡蠣フライやえびフライなどは、
日本の洋食としてすっかり定着しています。

作り方

① ボウルに水と塩少々を入れ、ざるに入れた牡蠣をつけて洗う 。

② ①の水気を拭き、塩、こしょうをふる。

③ ②に小麦粉を薄くまぶし、次に溶き卵をつける。

さらにパン粉をまぶし、手で軽くにぎる 。

④ 揚げ油を高温（180℃）に熱して③を少しずつ入れ、1〜2度返し、キツネ色になる一歩手前で取り出す 。

⑤ キッチンペーパーを敷いたバットに重ならないように並べて油をきる。

⑥ 器に盛り、キャベツのせん切りやクレソン、レモンを添え、ソースをかける。

Although fried foods originally came from the West,
fried oysters and shrimps are now very popular Japanese dishes.

DIRECTIONS

① Mix water with a pinch of salt in a large bowl. Put the oysters into a strainer, and wash while shaking through the strainer.

② Wipe excess water from ①, sprinkle with salt and pepper.

③ Dust ② with flour, then dip them into the beaten egg. Coat the oysters in breadcrumbs and squeeze lightly.

④ Heat the oil to high temperature (360°F), put a few ③ into the oil slowly, turn them over 1 or 2 times, then remove just before golden brown.

⑤ Drain excess oil by laying them on kitchen paper on a tray. Lay oysters side by side, don't stack them.

⑥ Serve oysters on plates, and garnish with shredded cabbage or watercress, eat with lemon juice and Worcester sauce.

Tonkatsu

とんカツ
Pork Cutlets

元は西洋料理のポーク・カツレツですが、
すっかり日本独自の料理としてアレンジされています。

下ごしらえ

材料（4人分）

豚ロース肉…4枚(400g)	とんかつソース……適量
塩・こしょう……各少々	練り辛子……少々
衣	
┌小麦粉……適量	
│溶き卵……1個分	
└パン粉……適量	
揚げ油……適量	
キャベツ……適量	
パセリ……適量	
ミニトマト……適量	

作り方

①豚肉は脂身に直角に包丁を入れて筋を切る（揚げたとき縮まないように）**Ⓐ**。

②軽く塩、こしょうをふり、小麦粉をまぶし、余分な粉を払い落とす**Ⓑ**。

③溶き卵をつけ、パン粉を全体にまぶす**Ⓒ**。

The Western dish of pork cutlets has become a thoroughly Japanese dish with a little change in the recipe.

Preparation

INGREDIENTS
(4 servings)

4 pork loin chops (14 oz)	cabbage to taste
salt and pepper to taste	parsley to taste
Batter	cherry tomatoes
┌wheat flour	to taste
│1 beaten egg	*tonkatsu* sauce to taste
└dried breadcrumbs	Japanese mustard
vegetable oil for frying	to taste

DIRECTIONS

① Make cuts into the fat at a right angle (to prevent shrinkage while deep-frying). **Ⓐ**

② Sprinkle both sides of the meat with a pinch of salt and pepper, dust with flour and shake off excess flour. **Ⓑ**

③ Dip the meat into the beaten egg and coat with the breadcrumbs entirely. **Ⓒ**

中温の油でじっくりと揚げ、豚肉の中までよく火を通します。
日本で生まれた、とんかつソースをかけていただきます。

揚げ方

①揚げ油を中温（170℃）に
熱する。
②豚肉を1枚入れ、その
後、少しずつ入れる（一度
に入れると油の温度が下が
り過ぎるので注意）。

③先に入れたものから1〜
2度返し、両面がこんがり
キツネ色になるまで、じっ
くり揚げて、中までよく火
を通す。
④揚げたてを食べやすく切

る。
⑤器に盛り、キャベツのせ
ん切りやパセリ、ミニトマ
ト、練り辛子を添え、とん
かつソースをかける。

Cook the pork slowly at medium heat to ensure that the meat is cooked thoroughly.
Serve with the uniquely Japanese *tonkatsu* sauce.

How to fry

① Heat the oil in a pan
to medium temperature
(340°F).
② Slide the meat into
the oil,  then continue
deep-frying slowly one
by one. (Be careful not
to put too many pieces
into the pan at one

time, as the oil temper-
ature will drop quickly.)
③ Turn the first over 1
or 2 times, fry slowly
until well cooked and
golden brown.
④ Cut the fried pork in-
to bite-sized pieces.
⑤ Serve on plates, gar-

nish with shredded ca-
bbage, parsley and
cherry tomatoes, and
add mustard and *tonka-
tsu* sauce.

ポ イ ン ト ー 1

ロース肉の代わりにフィレ肉を使うと脂身が少なく、さっぱりと仕上がります。

ポ イ ン ト ー 2

とんカツにひと手間かけると、カツ丼になります。だし汁1カップ、みりん・しょうゆ各大さじ3で、玉ねぎの薄切り½個分を煮、切ったとんカツ4枚分を入れ、溶き卵4個分を回し入れ、半熟状になったら火を止めます。ご飯にのせてグリーンピースを散らします。

カツ丼
Katsudon

POINT 1

Use pork fillet instead of loin for a lighter dish with less fat.

POINT 2

You can make *katsudon* easily with *tonkatsu*. Cook ½ sliced medium–sized onion with 1 cup *dashi* stock, 3 Tbsp *mirin* and 3 Tbsp soy sauce. Put cut pork cutlets (for 4 whole cutlets) on top and pour on 4 beaten egg in a circular motion. Simmer until the eggs are half cooked and turn off the heat. Pour onto cooked rice and add green peas.

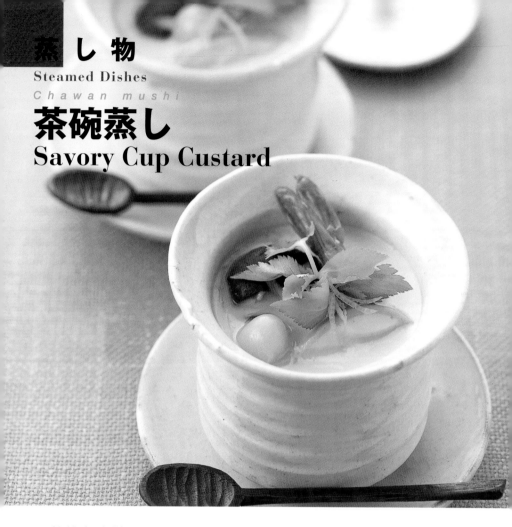

蒸し物
Steamed Dishes
Chawan mushi
茶碗蒸し
Savory Cup Custard

<table>
<tr><td>

材料（4人分）

えび……4尾
かまぼこ……4切れ
しいたけ……4個
ぎんなん……12粒
三つ葉……8本
塩……適量
卵液
┌ 卵……4個
│ だし汁……3カップ
│ 酒……小さじ1
│ 薄口しょうゆ……小さじ1
└ 塩……小さじ1
ゆずの皮……少々

</td><td>

INGREDIENTS (4 servings)

4 prawns
4 slices *kamaboko* (fish cake)
4 *shiitake* mushrooms
12 ginkgo nuts
8 strigs *mitsuba* (trefoil)
pinch of salt
Custard
┌ 4 eggs
│ 2½ U.S. cups *dashi* stock
│ 1 tsp *sake*
│ 1 tsp light soy sauce
└ 1 tsp salt
yuzu peel to taste

</td></tr>
</table>

薄味に調味した卵液に、淡白な具を加え、
ふた付きの茶碗に入れて蒸します。
つるんとした滑らかな食感に仕上げるのが、
おいしさのポイントです。

下ごしらえ

作り方

①えびは殻をむいて、背わたを取り（P55参照）、塩少々をふる。
②しいたけは石突きを除き、カサに飾り包丁を入れる

（P164参照）。
③ぎんなんは殻をむき、塩ゆでし、薄皮をむく。
④三つ葉は根を切り落とし、2本ずつ結ぶ。
⑤卵液を作る。鍋にだし汁

を煮立て、調味料を加えて冷ます。
⑥ボウルに卵をていねいに溶きほぐし、⑤を混ぜ、目の細かいざるでこす（滑らかな卵液にする）。

Tasty morsels are added to a subtly flavored egg custard
which is then steamed in a lidded teacup.
The key to this dish is the smoothness of the custard.

Preparation

DIRECTIONS

① Remove the shell and black vein from the prawns, (See P.55) sprinkle with a pinch of salt.
② Cut the stems off the *shiitake* mushrooms, score the heads with a cross. (See P.164)
③ Remove the hard shells of the ginkgo nuts, boil in salted water and remove the soft skins.
④ Cut the roots off the *mitsuba*, put two *mitsuba* stems together, and tie a knot.
⑤ Make the custard : Boil the *dashi* stock in a pan, add the seasonings, and cool.
⑥ Beat the eggs in a large bowl gently, add ⑤ and mix well, then strain through a fine sieve (this will keep the custard smooth).

ふた付きの茶碗がない場合は、ラップをかけて蒸します。
蒸すときの火の強さや時間が、仕上がりを左右します。

蒸し方

①器にえび、かまぼこ、しいたけ、ぎんなんを等分に入れる**Ⓐ**。
②卵液を等分に流し入れる**Ⓑ**。
③蒸し器に水を入れ、ふたをして強火にかける。蒸気が上がったら火を止め、②

にふたをして並べ入れる**Ⓒ**。
④蒸し器のふたをし**Ⓓ**、強火で2～3分蒸し、中火に近い弱火にして約20分蒸す（弱火すぎると具から水分が出て水っぽくなる。蒸し時間が長過ぎると固くなるので注意）。

⑤竹串を刺して、火の通り具合をみる**Ⓔ**。澄んだ汁が出れば取り出す。黄色い汁が出たら、さらに2～3分蒸す。
⑥取り出したら、三つ葉とゆずを入れて、ふたをする。

If teacups with lids are not available, use cling film and cups.
The duration and intensity of steaming are very important to the result.

How to steam

① Divide the prawn, fish cake, *shiitake* mushrooms and ginkgo nuts into serving cups.**Ⓐ**
② Pour the custard mixture into each cup.**Ⓑ**
③ Fill a steamer half full of water, cover with a lid, and bring to the boil over high heat. When it is steaming, turn off the heat, and then transfer ② with lids on to the steamer.**Ⓒ**
④ Cover the steamer, and steam on high for about 2 or 3 minutes, and then reduce the heat to medium-low, steam for about 20 minutes. (Take care. If the temperature is too low,

moisture will come out from the ingredients and the custard will be watery. If it's steamed for too long, the custard will go hard.)**Ⓓ**
⑤ Check by inserting a bamboo skewer into the custard. **Ⓔ** If a clear liquid emerges, it's done. But if yellow liquid

蒸し器
Steamer

蒸し皿
Steam tray

D **E**

comes out, steam for 2
or 3 minutes more.

⑥ Remove the cups fr-
om the steamer, gar-
nish with *mistuba* and
yuzu peel on top, then
cover each with a lid
and serve.

ぎんなん
Ginkgo nuts

松茸の土瓶蒸し
Matsutake Mushroom Pot Soup

材料（4人分）

松茸……2本
鶏ささ身……2本
えび……4尾
かまぼこ……8切れ
三つ葉……適量
汁
 ┌ だし汁……3カップ
 │ 塩……小さじ1
 └ 薄口しょうゆ……小さじ2
塩・酒……各適量
すだち……2個

INGREDIENTS (4 servings)

2 _matsutake_ mushrooms
2 pieces chicken white meat
4 prawns
8 slices _kamaboko_ (fish cake)
a little of _mitsuba_ (torefoil)
Soup
 ┌ 2½ U.S. cups _dashi_ stock
 │ 1 tsp salt
 └ 2 tsp light soy sauce
salt and _sake to taste_
2 _sudachi_

松茸
Matsutake
mushrooms

144

日本人の松茸好きは知られていますが、
中でも土瓶蒸しは香りを存分に味わえる、
代表的な料理です。

ポイント

土瓶の上に乗っている杯を取って汁を注ぎ、すだち少々を絞って飲みます。中の具はふたを開けて、適宜食べます。

作り方

①汁の材料を鍋に入れて強火にかけ、ひと煮立ちさせる。

②松茸は軽く洗い、根元の土のついている部分は包丁で削る。縦4つに裂いて、酒少々をふる。

③鶏肉はそぎ切りにして塩・酒各少々をふる。

④えびは殻をむいて背わたを取り(P55参照)、サッとゆでる。

⑤三つ葉はざく切りにする。

⑥器に②〜④とかまぼこを等分に入れ、①を注ぐ。

⑦蒸し器に⑥を入れて強火で10分、中火で10分蒸す。取り出して、三つ葉を加える。

⑧ふたをして、半分に切ったすだちを添える。

Japanese are famous for liking *matsutake* mushrooms, and this dish is a great one for revealing the unique fragrance of this mushroom.

DIRECTIONS

① Combine all the soup ingredients in a pan, and bring to the boil.

② Wash the *matsutake* mushrooms lightly, and shave off the end of the stalk.  Tear the *matsutake* mushrooms lengthwise into 4 pieces, and sprinkle with a little *sake*.

③ Slice the chicken, and sprinkle with salt and *sake*.

④ Remove the shell and black vein from the prawns and parboil.

⑤ Chop the *mitsuba* roughly.

⑥ Divide ② to ④ and fish cake among cups, and pour ① over.

⑦ Place ⑥ in a steamer, steam on high for 10 minutes, and then reduce the heat to medium, steam for 10 minutes. Remove the cups from the steamer, add *mitsuba*.

⑧ Cover each cup with a lid, and serve with *sudachi* cut in half.

145

あさりの酒蒸し
Sake-steamed Clams

お酒で蒸すだけのとても簡単な料理ですが、
あさりからだしが出て、味わい深さは抜群です。

材料（4人分）

あさり（殻付き）…600g
青ねぎ……適量
酒……⅔カップ

作り方

①あさりは3％濃度の塩水に2〜3時間つけて、砂を吐かせたあと、殻と殻をこすり合わせるようにして洗う。

②青ねぎはざく切りにする。

③浅鍋に①と酒を入れ、

ふたをして強火にかける。

④あさりの殻が開いたら、②を加え、汁ごと器に盛る。

Although simply steaming clams in *sake* is very easy to prepare, this is a very tasty dish with a rich clam flavor.

INGREDIENTS
(4 servings)

21 oz live hard shell short-necked clams
scallions to taste
½ U.S. cup *sake*

DIRECTIONS

① Soak the clams in salted water (water with 3% salt) for 2 or 3 hours to let them expel any sand, wash well by rubbing the shells against each other.

② Chop the scallions roughly.

③ Put ① and *sake* into a shallow pan, covered, and place over high heat.

④ When the clams open, add ② , and serve clams and juice in a bowl.

青ねぎ
Scallions

和え物

Kyuri to wakame no sunomono

きゅうりとわかめの酢の物

Vinegary Salad of
Cucumber and *Wakame*

材料を酢で和えた酢の物は、
口中をさっぱりとさせる副菜で、食欲をそそる効果もあります。

材料（4人分）

きゅうり……2本
わかめ(塩蔵)……50ｇ
三杯酢
　酢……大さじ3
　砂糖……大さじ1
　しょうゆ……小さじ1
　塩……少々

作り方

①きゅうりは薄い輪切りにする。

②わかめは水につけて戻し、水気を絞って食べやすく切り❹、①と合わせる。

③ボウルに三杯酢の材料を入れてよく混ぜ、②に加えて混ぜる❸。

④軽く汁気を絞って器に盛る❻。

This vinegar salad has two functions –it both refreshes the palate and stimulates the appetite.

INGREDIENTS
(4 servings)

2 cucumbers
2 oz salted *wakame* (seaweed)
Vinegar sauce(*sanbai-zu*)
　3 Tbsp vinegar
　1 Tbsp sugar
　1 tsp soy sauce
　salt to taste

DIRECTIONS

① Cut the cucumber into thin, round slices.

② Soak the *wakame* in water until soft, squeeze, cut into bite-sized pieces, ❹ then add to ①.

③ Mix well all the vinegar sauce ingredients in a bowl, add ②, then mix.❸

④ Squeeze lightly, serve in individual bowls.❻

しらす干し
Dried young sardines

いんげんのごま和え
Beans with Sesame Paste

黒ごまを使って和えたものは、
「材料を黒く汚す」という見た目から
「ごま汚し」と呼ばれることもあります。

材料（4人分）

いんげん……250 g
しょうゆ……少々
和え衣
┌黒ごま……大さじ3
│しょうゆ……大さじ1
│砂糖……大さじ1
└みりん……小さじ2

作り方

①いんげんはヘタを折り、そのまま引っ張って筋を取る**Ⓐ**。熱湯でゆでて水気をきり、しょうゆをふる。

②ごまは鍋に入れて弱火にかけ、ふっくらするまで空炒りする。

③②をすり鉢に取って、すりこ木ですり**Ⓑ**、和え衣の調味料を加えてすり混ぜる。

④①の汁気をきって③に加え、よく混ぜて器に盛る**Ⓒ**。

*Because dishes mixed with black sesame have
a blackened appearance,
they are also called Goma yogoshi.*

INGREDIENTS
(4 servings)

9 oz string beans
a dash of soy sauce
Sauce *(aegoromo)*
┌3 Tbsp black sesame
│ seeds
│1 Tbsp soy sauce
│1 Tbsp sugar
└2 tbsp *mirin*

DIRECTIONS

① Trim the string beans: Remove the strings and tops. **Ⓐ** Boil them, and squeeze out excess water, then add a few drops of soy sauce.

② Put the sesame seeds into a pan over low heat, toast until puffy.

③ Grind ② sesame seeds with a wooden pestle, **Ⓑ** add all the sauce seasonings, and then grind well.

④ Squeeze ① to remove liquid, add ③, and mix well. Serve in a bowl.**Ⓒ**

Shira-ae
白和え
White Salad

材料（4人分）

こんにゃく……½枚
にんじん……½本
いんげん……8本
煮汁
　┌だし汁……½カップ
　│しょうゆ……大さじ1
　│みりん……大さじ1
　└酒……大さじ1
和え衣
　┌木綿豆腐……½丁（150g）
　│白ごま……大さじ2
　│砂糖……大さじ1
　│薄口しょうゆ……大さじ1
　└塩……少々

INGREDIENTS (4 servings)

½ block *konnyaku*
½ carrot
8 string beans
Sauce
　┌½ U.S. cup *dashi* stock
　│1 Tbsp soy sauce
　│1 Tbsp *mirin*
　└1 Tbsp *sake*
Sauce(*aegoromo*)
　┌1 block *momendofu* (cotton *tofu*)
　│2 Tbsp white sesame seeds
　│1 Tbsp sugar
　└1 Tbsp light soy sauce
　pinch of salt

豆腐と白ごまを使って和えるので、
見た目が白くなるため、白和えといいます。
具には野菜を中心に使います。

作り方

①こんにゃくはゆでて短冊切りに、にんじんも短冊切りにする。いんげんはヘタと筋を除いて（P151参照）ゆで、斜め切りにする。

②鍋に煮汁と①を入れ、中火にかけて煮、汁がなく

なったら、ざるに取って冷ます。

③豆腐はサッとゆでて水きりする。白ごまは鍋で空炒りする。

④すり鉢で白ごまをすり、豆腐を加えてすり混ぜ、さらに和え衣の調味料を加

えてすり混ぜる。

⑤②を加えてよく混ぜる。

The white ingredients, such as *tofu* and white sesame seeds, give this dish its name *"shira-ae."* It is made with vegetables mainly.

DIRECTIONS

① Boil the *konnyaku*, cut into rectangles. Cut the carrot into rectangles also. Remove the string and tops from the green beans, (See P.151) boil and slice diagonally.

② Put ① and all the sauce ingredients into a

pan, place over medium heat.  Simmer until most of the liquid has gone. Strain and leave to cool.

③ Parboil the *tofu* and drain. Toast the white sesame seeds in a pan.

④ Grind the white sesame seeds in a grinder, add *tofu* and grind,

 then add all the sauce(*aegoromo*) ingredients,and grind well.

⑤ Add ②, and mix well.

菜の花の辛子和え

Nanohana with Mustard Sauce

ピリッと辛みがきいた和え物で、魚介や野菜によく合います。
春の素材の菜の花を使うと、季節感が出て味わいもひとしお。

菜の花は蕾のものと、やや花が開いたものと、どちらも使われます。独特の苦味がおいしく、ビタミンとミネラルが豊富。あさり、はまぐり、焼いた油揚げなどを加えてもおいしく仕上がります。とくに、はまぐりとの組み合わせは春らしく、ひな祭りの膳にもよく供されます。

菜の花
Nanohana

材 料（4人分）

菜の花……1把
和え衣
┌ しょうゆ…大さじ2
│ 練り辛子……小さじ1
└ だし汁……大さじ2

作り方

① 菜の花は根元を切り落とし、熱湯でゆでる。水にとって、水気を絞る。
② 3cm長さに切り、ギュッとにぎって水気を絞る**B**。
③ ボウルに和え衣の材料を入れてよく混ぜ、②を加えて混ぜ合わせる**C**。

This *aegoromo* is a little hot, so it goes well with seafood and vegetables. Use spring *Nanohana* and enjoy the seasonal taste of the ingredients.

There are two types of *nanohana*, buds and little blossoms, and you can use both types. *nanohana* is tasty, but it has a unique bitterness, and contains many vitamins and minerals. This dish is also delicious if you add short-neck clams, large clams or grilled deep-fried *tofu* (*abura-age*). Clams go particularly well with this dish. It is a harbinger of spring, and is often served at the Doll's Festival.

INGREDIENTS
(4 servings)

1 bunch *nanohana*
  (rapeseed)
Sauce (*aegoromo*)
┌ 2 Tbsp soy sauce
│ 2 tbsp
│   Japanese mustard
└ 2 Tbsp *dashi* stock

DIRECTIONS

① Cut the roots off the *nanohana*, and boil.**A** Rinse in water, and squeeze.
② Cut ① into 1.5-inch lengths, and squeeze out any excess water.**B**
③ Mix together all the sauce ingredients, add ②, and mix well.**C**

青柳とわけぎのぬた
Clams and Leeks with *Miso* Dressing

ぬたは、酢みそ和えのことです。
貝やねぎのほか、まぐろ、いか、わかめなども
よく用いられます。

材料（4人分）

青柳……200 g
わけぎ……4本
酢……少々
和え衣
　白みそ……大さじ2
　砂糖……大さじ½
　だし汁……大さじ2
　酢……大さじ1

作り方

①鍋に和え衣の材料を入れて弱火にかけ、混ぜてみそを溶かす。冷蔵庫で冷やす。

②青柳はざるに入れて振り洗いし、ざるごと熱湯にサッとつける。水にとって水気をきり、酢少々をふる（貝の生臭さを消す）。

③わけぎは熱湯でサッとゆでて、水気をきり、ざく切りにする。

④①、②、③を合わせて、よく混ぜる。

青柳
Aoyagi

Nuta means to mix with *miso* dressing.
Nuta dishes usually contain clams and leeks,
but tuna, squid and *wakame* can also be substituted.

INGREDIENTS
(4 servings)

7 oz *aoyagi* clams
4 *wakegi* leeks
pinch of vinegar
Sauce (*aegoromo*)
　2 Tbsp white *miso*
　½ Tbsp sugar
　2 Tbsp *dashi* stock
　1 Tbsp vinegar

DIRECTIONS

① Put all the sauce ingredients in a pan, place over low heat, and mix to dissolve the *miso*. Then cool in a refrigerator.

② Put surf clams in a sieve, wash them by shaking the clams together under running water. Then plunge the clams in the sieve into boiling water. Rinse them in water, shake out the water, and sprinkle with vinegar (to remove any briny odor from the clams).

③ Parboil the *wakegi*, drain and chop roughly.

④ Mix well ①, ② and ③.

すき焼き
Sukiyaki

材料（4人分）

牛ロース薄切り肉…600 g
焼き豆腐……1丁
長ねぎ……2本
春菊……½把
しらたき……1袋
牛脂……適量
割り下
　酒・みりん……各½カップ
　砂糖……大さじ2
　しょうゆ……¼カップ
卵……適量

INGREDIENTS (4 servings)

21 oz thinly sliced beef
1 block *yakidofu* (grilled *tofu*)
2 leeks
½ bunch *shungiku*
1 pack *shirataki*
beef lard to taste
Sauce (*warishita*)
　½ U.S. cup *sake*
　½ U.S. cup *mirin*
　2 Tbsp sugar
　⅕ U.S. cup soy sauce
eggs to taste

外国でも名高いすき焼きは、
牛肉や野菜などを焼いて
甘辛く調味した鍋物の一種です。

作り方

①割り下を作る。鍋に酒とみりんを入れて強火にかけ、沸騰したらしょうゆと砂糖を加え、砂糖を溶かす。
②焼き豆腐は一口大に、長ねぎは斜め切りにする。春菊は葉先を摘む。しらたき

はサッとゆでて、食べやすく切る。
③鉄鍋を熱して牛脂を溶かし、脂を広げる**Ａ**。
④牛肉適量を入れて焼き、①の割り下適量を注いでからめる**Ｂ**。
⑤②の具を入れて焼き**Ｃ**、

溶いた卵につけて食べる。具と割り下を適宜加えて焼く。

 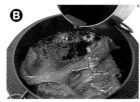 

すき焼き鍋
Sukiyaki-nabe

The world-famous *sukiyaki* is a Japanese hot pot with grilled beef and vegetables seasoned with soy sauce and sugar.

DIRECTIONS

① Make the sauce: Put the *sake* and *mirin* in a pan, place over high heat, bring to the boil, add soy sauce and sugar, and cook until the sugar is dissolved.
② Cut the *yakidofu* into bite-size pieces, and cut the leeks diagonally. Pick just the leaves of *shungiku*. Parboil *shirataki*, cut into bite-size pieces.
③ Heat an iron pan, melt the beef lard and spread over the pan.**Ａ**
④ Grill some beef in the pan, add some ① and coat the beef with it.**Ｂ**
⑤ Add ② and grill **Ｃ**. Eat by dipping the beef

in a beaten egg. Add the other ingredients and *warishita*, and grill.

しゃぶしゃぶ
Shabu-shabu

材料（4人分）

牛ロース薄切り肉……800 g
長ねぎ……2本
白菜……4枚
しいたけ……4個
えのきだけ……1袋
青ねぎ……1把
煮汁
  ┌ 水……8カップ
  └ 昆布……10cm
ポン酢しょうゆ……適量
ごまだれ
  ┌ だし汁……1カップ
  ├ 練り白ごま……大さじ5
  └ しょうゆ……大さじ4

INGREDIENTS (4 servings)

28 oz thinly sliced beef sirloin
2 leeks
4 leaves Chinese cabbage
4 *shiitake* mushrooms
1 pack of *enoki* mushrooms
1 bunch scallions
Sauce
  ┌ $6\frac{2}{3}$ U.S.cups water
  └ 4 inches *konbu* (kelp)
citrus dipping sauce (*ponzu*)
  to taste
Sesame dipping sauce (gomadare)
  ┌ 1 U.S. cup *dashi* stock
  ├ 5 Tbsp white sesame paste
  └ 4 Tbsp soy sauce

ごく薄切りにした上質の牛肉を、
湯の中でサッとゆがいて食べる鍋料理です。
ポン酢しょうゆとごまだれを用意します。

作り方

①長ねぎは斜め切り、白菜
と青ねぎはざく切りにす
る。しいたけは石突きを切
る。えのきだけは石突きを
切ってほぐす**Ⓐ**。
②ごまだれの材料を混ぜ合
わせる。

③鍋に煮汁の材料を入れ、
約20分おいて強火にかけ、
沸騰直前で昆布を取り出し
（入れたままでもよい）、中
火にする。
④各自、箸で牛肉を１枚ず
つはさみ、②の鍋につけて
サッサッとふる**Ⓑ**。

⑤色が変わったら、ポン酢
しょうゆやごまだれにつけ
て食べる**Ⓒ**。①は適宜入れ
て火を通す。

This *nabe* dish is made by dipping very thinly sliced,
high-quality beef into boiling water. Prepare
two different dipping sauces of *ponzu* and *gomadare*.

DIRECTIONS

① Cut leeks diagonally,
chop Chinese cabbage
and scallious roughly.
Remove the hard tips
from the *shiitake* mush-
rooms. Remove the
hard tips from the *enoki*
mushroom, and break
apart.**Ⓐ**
② Mix all the sesame
dipping sauce ingredi-
ents together.
③ Put all of the sauce
ingredients into a pan,

leave for about 20min-
utes. Place over high
heat, and remove the
konbu before it boils(as
it is), and then cook on
medium heat.
④ Each person takes
one slice of beef with
chopsticks, dips it into
the pan and shakes it.
Ⓑ
⑤ When the beef chan-
ges color, dip it into
your favorite dipping
sauce, and eat.**Ⓒ** Add

① to the pan and cook.

寄せ鍋
Yosenabe

魚介、肉、野菜など、
好きなものをいろいろ寄せ集めて
入れるので、寄せ鍋といいます。
ぐつぐつ煮ながら食べるので、
体の芯から温まる、冬の料理です。

材料（4人分）

えび……8尾
たら……4切れ
はまぐり……8個
鶏もも肉……200g
絹ごし豆腐……1丁
白菜……4枚
しいたけ……4個
長ねぎ……2本
にんじん……½本
春菊……1把

煮汁
　水……7カップ
　昆布……10cm
　みりん……¼カップ
　しょうゆ……¼カップ
　塩……小さじ1
薬味
　七味唐辛子……少々

にんじんとしいたけの飾り切り
Carved carrot and *shiitake* mushroom

土鍋
Clay pot

Yosenabe is so called because it combines all your favorite seafood, meat and vegetables altogether in a pot. It can be cooked and eaten at the table. It's a meal for the winter, as the piping hot stew warms you up.

INGREDIENTS (4 servings)

8 prawns
4 cod fillets
8 live clams
7 oz chicken thighs
1 block *kinugoshidofu* (smooth *tofu*)
4 leaves Chinese cabbage
4 *shiitake* mushrooms
2 leeks
½ carrot
1 bunch *shungiku*

Sauce
　6 U.S. cups water
　4 inches *konbu* (kelp)
　⅕ U.S. cup *mirin*
　⅕ U.S. cup soy sauce
　1 tsp salt
Condiments
　shichimi togarashi to taste

POINT

Yosenabe uses a clay pot. It allows gentle cooking and yet retains the heat well. If there is any soup leftover, you can enjoy cooking noodles and *zosui*. (See P.54)

材料の下ごしらえ

作り方
① えびは背わたを取る（殻からうまみが出るので殻はむかない）。
② はまぐりは砂出しして洗う（P35参照）。
③ たら、鶏肉、豆腐は一口大に切る。
④ 長ねぎは斜め切り、白菜はざく切りにする。
⑤ にんじんは薄い輪切りにして型で抜く。
⑥ しいたけは石突きを除いて、カサに飾り包丁を入れる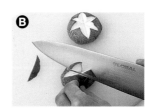。
⑦ 春菊は葉先を手でちぎり、茎を除く。

Ⓐ

Ⓑ

Ⓒ

Preparation

DIRECTIONS
① Remove the black vein from prawns. (Leave the shells on, as they will enhance the flavor.)
② Soak the clams to expel any sand, and wash. (See P.35)
③ Cut the cod, chicken and *tofu* into bite-size pieces.
④ Cut leeks diagonally, and chop Chinese cabbage roughly.
⑤ Cut carrots into thin round slices, and then cut into flower shapes with a Japanese vegetable cutter.Ⓐ
⑥ Remove the hard tips from the *shiitake* mushrooms, and cut a shallow slice into the top of each.Ⓑ
⑦ Remove the stem from the *shungiku*.Ⓒ

煮汁が煮立ったら具を適宜入れ、煮えたところから
各自、煮汁ごと取り分けていただきます。

作り方

①土鍋に水と昆布を入れ、約20分おいて強火にかけ、沸騰直前で昆布を取り出す（入れたままでもよい）。

②調味料を加えて、ひと煮立ちしたら弱火にする **D**。

③具適量を並べ入れて **E**、強火にし、煮立ったら弱火にする。

④火が通ったものから、煮汁ごと取り分け、好みで七味唐辛子をふって食べる **F**。

⑤残りの具は適宜加える。煮汁が少なくなったらお湯を足す。

When the sauce is boiling, put all the ingredients into the pot.
Each person picks out ingredients as they are cooked.

Directions

① Put the water and *konbu* into a clay pot (*donabe*), and leave for about 20 minutes. Place over high heat and remove the *konbu* just before the water boils (or leave the *konbu* in).

② Add the other sauce ingredients, bring back to the boil, and reduce the heat to low. **D**

③ Add some ingredients to the pot carefully **E**, cook at high heat until it boils, and then reduce the heat to low.

④ Serve the cooked ingredients with some soup, sprinkle with *shichimi togarashi*, if you like. **F**

⑤ Add the remaining ingredients to the pot. If there isn't enough sauce, add hot water.

Yudofu
湯豆腐
Tofu Hot Pot

材料（4人分）

絹ごし豆腐……2丁
煮汁
- 水……8カップ
- 昆布……20㎝
- 塩……少々

つけだれ
- 昆布だし汁……1カップ
- しょうゆ……大さじ4
- かつお節……適量

薬味
- 長ねぎの小口切り…適量
- 七味唐辛子……少々
- ゆずの皮……少々

INGREDIENTS (4 servings)

2 blocks *kinugoshidofu* (smooth *tofu*)
Sauce
- $6\frac{2}{3}$ U.S. cups water
- 8 inches *konbu* (kelp)
- pinch of salt

Dipping sauce (*tsukedare*)
- 1 U.S. cup *konbu dashi* stock
- 4 Tbsp soy sauce
- *katsuo-bushi* (bonito flakes) to taste

Condiments
- chopped leeks to taste
- *shichimi togarashi* to taste
- *yuzu* peel to taste

夏の冷奴に対し、冬は鍋で豆腐を煮ながら食べます。
かつお節を加えたしょうゆ味のたれを、鍋の中央で温めます。

作り方

①鍋に水と昆布を入れ、約20分おいて強火にかけ、沸騰したら火を止める（昆布は入れたままにする）。

②①を1カップ取り分け、しょうゆとかつお節を加えてつけだれを作り、器に入れて、鍋の中央に置く。

③鍋に塩を加えて強火にし、適宜切った豆腐を入れ**Ｂ**、煮立ったら弱火にして温める。

④各自、豆腐を②のたれにつけて**Ｃ**、小皿に取り分け、薬味を加えて食べる。

ポイント

豆腐からはだしが出ないので、昆布は入れたままにします。コンロに鍋をのせ、熱しながら食べるのも一般的です。豆腐に火を通し過ぎると固くなるので注意。煮汁に塩少々を加えることで、固くなるのを防げます。

Cold *tofu hiyayakko* is eaten in the summer, but in the cold winter season people eat hot *tofu* cooked in a pot. A container of soy sauce with *katsuo-bushi* is placed in the center of the pot to keep hot.

DIRECTIONS

① Put *konbu* and water in a pot, and leave for about 20 minutes. Place over high heat, and when it comes to the boil, turn off the heat. (Don't remove *konbu*.)

② Make the *tsukedare*; Set aside 1 cup *dashi* stock from ①, add the soy sauce and *katsuo-bushi*. Pour into a cup, **Ａ** and place in the center of the pot.

③ Add salt to the pot over high heat, add bite-sized pieces of *tofu*, **Ｂ** then reduce heat to low and keep warm.

④ Dip the *tofu* in ②, and eat with individual condiments. **Ｃ**

POINT

Tofu does not produce stock, so leave the *konbu* in the pot while cooking. Since *tofu* does not need much cooking, you can eat it while it's cooking on a portable gas stove. If you cook *tofu* for a long time, it will harden. Put a pinch of salt into the pot to prevent this.

弁当 *Bento*

容器におかずや主食を詰め合わせたものを弁当と
いいます。主に外出先で食べます。
A *bento* is a lunch box filled with various dishes and snacks.
It is common for people to bring them
whenever they have to eat away from home.

最も日常的な弁当は、学生や会社員な
どが持っていく手製のもので、弁当箱に
家で作った料理やご飯などを詰め合わせ
ます。

お花見やハイキングなどの行楽には、
大人数で食べられるよう、いくつものお
重などに、たくさんの料理を華やかに盛
りつけて持って行くこともあります。

お弁当は持参するだけでなく、外出先
で買う楽しみもあります。「駅弁」がそ

の代表的なもので、旅行には欠かせませ
ん。芝居の幕間に買って食べる「幕の内
弁当」や、料亭のランチメニューによく
ある「会席弁当」など、ぜいたくなもの
もあります。現在では、幕の内弁当とい
うと、多種類のおかずを詰めた高級感の
あるものを指すようになりました。

また、弁当は手軽な食事なので、コン
ビニや町の弁当屋などで購入し、家で食
べることも普通になりました。

The most common form of *bento* is
the home-made lunchbox carried
by students and office workers.
The box contains rice and other
dishes prepared at home.
There are also multi-tiered *bento*
boxes with a large variety of dishes suitable for many people. These
are used for trips such as flower
viewing parties or hiking outings.
It's also fun to buy a *bento* while
out, rather than bring your own.
Ekiben (station lunch boxes) are
the most common of these, and
are an integral part of many jour-
neys. There are also luxurious

家庭で作る手製の弁当。
ナプキンに包んで持って行きます。
Home made *bento*.
It is wrapped in a serviette
for takeout.

会席風のぜいたくな弁当。
This is a gourmet lunchbox, *kaiseki* style.

lunch boxes such as the *maku-nouchi bento* (interval lunchbox) enjoyed by theatergoers during the interval at a stage play, and the *kaiseki bento* served at lunch at expensive Japanese restaurants. Today, *makunouchi* has become a general term for any lunchbox containing a rich variety of gourmet items.

It's also common to buy *bento* from local convenience stores or *bento-ya* (takeout lunchbox restaurants) to eat at home.

お弁当グッズ
Bento goods

弁当箱
Bento box

プラスチックの
カップ
Plastic cup

箸箱
Chopsticks box

仕切り
Dividers

しょうゆなどを
入れる容器
Small bottle for soy sauce, etc.

まんじゅう
Sweet Bun

和菓子の代表的なもので、小麦粉などで作った皮で
あんを包み、蒸してふっくらとさせます。
そのバリエーションは日本全国に数限りなくありますが、
ここでは一番シンプルなものを紹介します。

皮の作り方

材料（4人分）

皮
- 砂糖……50 g
- 小麦粉……100 g
- 重曹……小さじ⅔
こしあん（缶詰）……200 g
小麦粉……適量

作り方

①鍋に砂糖と水50ccを入れ
て中火にかけ、砂糖を溶か
して冷ます。

②ボウルに小麦粉と①を入
れ、重曹を水大さじ1で溶

いて加え、へらでさっくり
と混ぜ合わせる❹。

③まな板に打ち粉をし（小
麦粉少々をふり）、その上
で②を棒状にまとめる❸。

④12等分に切る❻。

Manju is a typical *wagashi* (Japanese sweet).
It consists of sweet red beans wrapped in dough made from flour,
then steamed until fluffy. There are many variations of *manju*
from all over Japan, but this is the simplest one.

How to make the bun

INGREDIENTS
(4 servings)

BUN
- 2 oz sugar
- 3½ oz wheat flour
- ⅔ Tbsp baking soda
7 oz *koshian*
(tin of sweet red-bean
paste)
wheat flour

DIRECTIONS

① Put sugar and 50cc
water in a pan over
medium heat until the
sugar dissolves, then
leave to cool.

② Put flour and ① in a
bowl, add baking soda
with 1 Tbsp water, mix
roughly with a spatula.

❹

③ Sprinkle on a pinch
of flour over the chop-
ping board, put on ②.
Roll the dough, and
make a bar.❸

④ Cut into 12 portions.

❻

蒸す前は直径3cm程度の小さなものですが、
蒸し上がると、その倍ぐらいに、ふんわりと丸くなります。

作り方

①両手のひらに小麦粉少々をつけ、皮1個を取って丸める**A**。
②中央を押しつぶして、あんの1/12量を丸めてのせる**B**。
③皮で包み**C**、3cm角に切った経木（またはオーブンシート）の上に、合わせ目を下にして置く。同様に11個作る。
④蒸気の上がった蒸し器（P142参照）に、③を間隔をあけて並べて入れる**D**。
⑤ふたをして、強火で7～8分蒸す。

Before steaming, the sweet bun is only 1.5-inches in diameter.
After steaming, the bun swells to twice its size and becomes fluffy and round.

Directions

① Sprinkle flour over both hands, take one piece of dough and roll into a ball.**A**
② Press a hollow into the center of the dough, put a small pellet (1/12th) of the *koshian* into the dough. **B**
③ Cover the *koshian* with the dough, **C** and put the bun (with the joint facing down) onto a 1.5-inch square *kyougi* (or oven sheet). Make the other 11 buns in the same way.
④ When the steamer is steaming, (See P.142) place ③ evenly apart on the steamer. **D**

172

ようかん
Yokan

らくがん
Rakugan

⑤ Cover with the lid, and steam over high heat for about 7 or 8 minutes.

POINT 1

An (sweet-bean paste) is beans cooked with sugar. Dark brown *azuki* beans are used typically. There are two different types; *tsubu-an*, with some beans still whole, and *koshi-an*, a smooth paste. Choose whichever type you prefer.

POINT 2

Wagashi can be divided in two types, fresh *nama-gashi* and dry *hi-gashi*. The sweet bun (*manju*) and dumpling (*dango*) belong to the fresh *nama-gashi* type. *Wagashi* with below 10% water are called *hi-gashi*, and there are many different types such as *yokan*, made from sweet red beans and *kanten* jelly, and *rakugan*, made from wheat flour and sugar.

Kushi dango

串団子
Skewered Dumplings

<table>
<tr><td>

材料（4人分）

上新粉……200 g
白玉粉……40 g
たれ
  ┌ しょうゆ……大さじ 2
  │ 砂糖……大さじ 4
  │ 片栗粉……小さじ 1
  └ 水……小さじ 2
あん（缶詰）……適量

</td><td>

INGREDIENTS (4 servings)

7 oz *joshinko* (non-glutinous rice flour)
1½ oz *shiratamako* (glutinous rice flour)
Sauce
  ┌ 2 Tbsp soy sauce
  │ 4 Tbsp sugar
  │ 1 tsp *katakuriko* (starch)
  └ 2 tsp water
koshian (tin of sweet red-bean paste) to tast

</td></tr>
</table>

174

団子は、米粉である上新粉や、
もち米粉である白玉粉など使い、
小さく丸めて蒸したものです。

作り方

①ボウルに上新粉、白玉粉、ぬるま湯¾カップを入れて混ぜ、ひとつにまとめる。

②蒸気の上がった蒸し器に濡れ布巾を敷き、①を適当にちぎって入れる 。

③ふたをして強火で約20分蒸し、水にとって冷ます。

④濡れ布巾にとり、布巾の上からよくもんで、なめらかな生地を作る 。

⑤④を2cm太さの棒状にして2cm幅に切り、1つずつ丸めて竹串に刺す 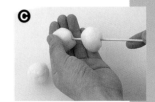。

⑥小鍋にたれの材料を入れて中火にかけ、かき混ぜながらひと煮立ちさせる。

⑦⑤の半量に、⑥のたれを塗る。

⑧⑤の残りにあんをのせる。

Dango (dumpling) is a small steamed ball of
joshinko (non-glutinous rice flour) or
shiratamako (glutinous rice flour).

DIRECTIONS

① Mix the *joshinko*, *shiratamako* and ⅗ U.S. cup lukewarm water in a bowl and knead into a dough.

② When the steamer is steaming, spread a wet cloth inside, tear ① into small pieces and place in the steamer.

③ Cover with a lid, steam over high heat for about 20 minutes, and then put into water.

④ Wrap the dough in a wet cloth, rub well until smooth.

⑤ Make ④ into a 1-inch diameter stick, then cut into 1-inch lengths. Roll each piece into a ball, and bamboo skewer them.

⑥ Put all the sauce ingredients into a small pan, place over medium heat, stir with a spatula until boiling.

⑦ Brush ⑥ on both sides of the skewered dumplings.

⑧ Put *koshian* onto the remaining dumplings.

会 席 料 理 *Kaiseki* Cuisine

日本の祝いの席やあらたまった宴席などに供される料理で、
洋食の正式なディナーにあたります。
Kaiseki cuisine is usually presented at celebrations
or formal occasions in Japan, and corresponds
to formal dinner party cuisine in the West.

　正式なディナーのメニューに決まりがあるように、会席料理の献立にも決まりがあります。

　一般的には、お通しから始まって、刺身、煮物、吸い物、焼き物、揚げ物、蒸し物、和え物などの順に一品ずつ供され、最後にご飯とみそ汁、香の物（漬け物）が出て、くだものや菓子とお茶で締めくくります。

　少しくだけた宴席や旅館の食事など

では、一品ずつ供されるのではなく、これらの料理が一度にずらりと並べられます。

　会席料理には、通常はお酒がつきもので、ご飯が出るまで、これらの料理を肴にして日本酒などを飲みます。

　ちなみに、「懐石料理」は音が同じですが別物で、こちらは茶の湯に伴う食事で、献立や作法に厳格な決まりがあります。

Just as in Western formal dinners, *Kaiseki* cuisine has many rules concerning the menu.

Usually, the meal begins with *otoushi* (amuse bouche), and continues with *sashimi* (raw fish), *nimono* (simmered dish), *suimono* (soup), *yakimono* (grilled dish), *agemono* (deepfried-dish), *mushimono* (steamed dish), *aemono* (salad), in that order. The meal ends with rice and *miso* soup, *tsukemono* (pickles) and finally fruit, dessert and tea.

With more informal parties or venues, the dishes are not presented one by one but all the dishes are laid out on the table from the beginning.

Kaiseki cuisine is usually accompanied by alcoholic beverages until the rice course, and these dishes go well with Japanese *sake*.

There is another version of *kaiseki* cuisine with the tea ceremony, but its rules and regulations are very strict.

日本食の基礎知識

日本の食材、調味料、調理道具、器、マナーについて、
知っておきたい基本的なことを解説しています。
日本食をより深く理解するためのミニ事典です。

Chapter 3
Basics of Japanese Cuisine

This chapter explains all you should know about Japanese food,
aspices, cooking utensils, tableware, and table manners.
It's a little dictionary to enable you to
better understand Japanese cuisine.

日本の食材
Japanese Foods

いろいろな料理に日ごろよく使われる
主な食材を紹介します。

Many of the foods commonly used in Japanese cooking are introduced here.

昆布

海藻の一種で、干してあり、だしをとるのに使います。昆布だけでとるだしは旨みが柔らかで上品な味わい。

KONBU (KELP)

This dried seaweed is often used for making stock. A stock made solely from *konbu* has a subtle and sophisticated taste.

わかめ

海藻の一種。生（右）、塩蔵（中央）、乾燥（左）があります。塩蔵品と乾燥品は水につけて戻してから使います。

WAKAME (SEAWEED)

A type of seaweed, available fresh (right), salted (center) or dried (left). Salted or dried varieties should be softened by soaking in water before use.

かつお節（削り節）

かつおなどを乾燥させて削ったもの。旨みが強いので昆布と合わせてだしをとったり、料理にふりかけたりします。

KATSUO-BUSHI (BONITO FLAKES)

Shavings of dried fish such as bonito. *Katsuo-bushi* has quite a strong flavor and is therefore often used with *konbu* for stock, or sprinkled over a dish.

のり

海藻の一種で、薄く延ばして干したもの。そのまま適当な大きさに切ったり、ちぎったりして使い、主に香りを楽しみます。

NORI (SEAWEED)

A type of seaweed, dried in thin sheets. It is used as it is, cut or torn into pieces. It is popular mainly for its aroma.

豆腐

大豆を加工したもので、植物性たんぱく質がとれます。食感の違いで、絹ごし豆腐と木綿豆腐があります。(P99参照)

TOFU

A form of vegetable protein derived from processed soybeans. Comes in different textures, such as silky smooth or coarse. (See P.99)

かまぼこ

魚肉を加工したもので、板に半月状に付いています。切ってそのまま食べてもいいし、汁物や温かい麺の具などにします。

KAMABOKO (FISH CAKE)

Processed fish that comes in various shapes. It can be sliced and eaten as it is, or added to hot noodles or soups.

油揚げ・焼き豆腐

どちらも豆腐の加工品。油揚げ(上)は豆腐を薄く切って揚げたもの。焼き豆腐(下)は両面を焼いたものです。

ABURA-AGE / YAKIDOFU

Two variations of processed *tofu*. *Abura-age* (top) is thin slices of *tofu* deep fried. *Yakidofu* (bottom) is *tofu* that has been roasted on both sides.

そば・うどん・そうめん

日本の麺は、そばから作るそば(左)と、小麦から作るうどん(中央)に大別されます。そうめん(右)はうどんの一種で極細のもの。いずれも、ゆでて冷やしたり、温かい汁に入れたり、冷・温どちらの食べ方もあります。

SOBA / UDON / SOMEN NOODLES

Japanese noodles can be roughly divided into *soba* (left) made from buckwheat and *udon* (center) made from wheat. *Somen* (right) is a kind of very thin *udon*, or Japanese vermicelli. All can be eaten cold or hot, cooked and dipped in cold sauce or added to hot soup.

春菊

菊の葉に似た形状と香りをもつ青菜。おひたしや和え物などに用いられるほか、鍋物には欠かせない香味野菜です。

SHUNGIKU (SPRING CHRYSANTHEMUM)

A green leaf that has the look and aroma of chrysanthemum. It is often used in boiled vegetables and salads, etc., and is always added to *nabemono* for extra flavor.

三つ葉

香りがいいので、葉、茎とも薬味として利用されます。煮物、汁物、蒸し物などにサッと火を通してあしらわれます。

MITSUBA (TREFOIL)

Mitsuba has a lovely aroma, and the stems and leaves are used whole. It should be quickly cooked and added to stews, soups and steamed dishes.

しいたけ・えのきだけ

どちらもきのこ類で、煮物、鍋物、炒め物など幅広く使われます。しいたけ（上）には干ししいたけもあります。同じきのこ類のまつたけは希少価値の高価なもので、旬の秋にだけ出回ります。

SHIITAKE MUSHROOMS / ENOKIDAKE MUSHROOMS

Both these mushrooms are widely used in *nabe-mono*, simmered or fried dishes. *Shiitake* are also available dried. Another mushroom, the *matsu-take*, is only available in the fall, and is expensive because of its rarity.

長ねぎ・青ねぎ・わけぎ

長ねぎ（上）はいろいろな料理に、または薬味として、非常によく用いられます。主に白い部分を使います。青ねぎは葉の部分を使う細いねぎで、主に薬味に用いられます。極細のあさつき（中央）と、やや太い万能ねぎがあります。わけぎ（下）はねぎの変種で、柔らかくて甘みがあり、ぬたなどに使われます。

LEEK / SCALLION / WAKEGI

The white part of leeks (top) is used in many dishes, or as a condiment to others. The leaf of the thin *asatsuki* (center) scallions is used as a condiment, like the *ban-nonegi*, a slightly thicker scallions. *Wakegi* (bottom) is a peculiar leek, both soft and sweet, is used in *nuta*.

青じそ

和製バジルともいわれる爽やかな香りがあり、生のまま刺身のツマや薬味として用いたり、天ぷらのタネにすることもあります。

AO-JISO

Also known as Japanese basil, this has a refreshing taste and is used fresh as a condiment or decoration for *sashimi* dishes, or deep-fried with *tempura*, etc.

えのきだけ
Enokidake mushrooms

絹さや

グリーンピースの未熟なもので、さやごと食べます。サッとゆでて、煮物などのあしらいによく使われます。

KINUSAYA (SNOW PEAS)

These are young green peas and are eaten pod and all. They are boiled quickly and used to garnish other dishes.

ゆず・すだち

ともに柑橘類。香りと酸味が強いので汁を料理に絞ったり、皮は細かく刻んで薬味にします。ゆず（左）は香りに甘みがあり、すだち（右）の香りはすっきりしています。

YUZU / SUDACHI

Two citrus fruits. Because of their pungent aroma and sour taste, only the juice is used, or thinly sliced peel as a condiment. *Yuzu* (left) has a sweet aroma, while *sudachi* (right) has a fresh scent.

黒ごま・白ごま

料理の彩りに合わせて使い分けます。消化・吸収をよくし、臭みを除くために必ず空炒りします。それをすりつぶして和え物などに使ったりします。

BLACK AND WHITE SESAME

The different colors of sesame are used according to the dish. It is good for the digestion. Always cook in a pan without oil to soften the harsh flavor of sesame. Sesame can be ground up, or used as it is in salads.

みょうが

夏が旬の香味野菜の一種。生のまま薬味として用いたり、酢の物や汁物などに加えたりします。

MYOUGA

An aromatic summer vegetable. It is used fresh as a condiment, or added to soups or pickled dishes.

木の芽

山椒の若葉。独特の強い芳香があるので、生のまま煮物などのあしらいに。実も薬味として利用します。

BUDS

Young leaf buds of the Japanese pepper tree. These are used for their unique fragrance – either raw in cooked dishes or as condiments.

日本の調味料
料理の味つけに使うもののほか、製品化された薬味調味料もあわせて紹介します。

Japanese Seasonings
This section introduces the various seasonings used in Japanese cooking, including processed condiments.

しょうゆ
通常使われる「濃口しょうゆ」(左)と、色を薄く仕上げたいときに使う「薄口しょうゆ」(右)があります。

SOY SAUCE
Dark soy sauce (left) is most commonly used, but light soy sauce (right) is also used for coloring.

酒
日本酒のこと。料理用がありますが、飲用を使ってもOK。

SAKE
Japanese liquor. It can be used for cooking, but can also be drunk on its own.

みそ
一般的な「信州みそ」(左)のほか、「赤みそ」(右上)と「白みそ」(右下)があります(P 33参照)。

MISO
Apart from the common Shinshu miso (left), there are also red (right-top) and white (right-bottom) varieties. (See P.33)

みりん
甘みのついた酒で、料理に甘み、旨み、つやを与える効果があります。

MIRIN
A sweet sake, this is used in cooking to add flavor, sweetness and gloss.

酢
西洋のビネガーのように果実の香りがない、さっぱりとした酸味。米酢と穀物酢があり、米酢のほうが上質。

VINEGAR
This lacks the fruity aroma of Western vinegar, and has a light sourness. It can be made from rice or cereals, but rice vinegar is more refined.

ポン酢しょうゆ

しょうゆにゆずなどの汁を加えたもので、鍋物のたれとしてよく使われます。

PONZU

Soy sauce with *yuzu* juice, etc., added. Often used as a dipping sauce for *nabemono*.

とんかつソース・中濃ソース

「とんかつソース」（左）は、西洋のサラサラのウスターソースが、とんカツ用に濃厚にアレンジされたもの。両者の中間が「中濃ソース」（右）。

TONKATSU SAUCE / CHUNO SAUCE

Tonkatsu sauce (left), a thicker variant of Worcester sauce, is eaten with pork cutlets. *Chuno* sauce (right) is in between *tonkatsu* and Worcester.

インスタントだし

顆粒状で、お湯に溶くだけで、だしが作れます。

INSTANT *DASHI* STOCK

Simply dissolve the granules in hot water to make stock.

七味唐辛子

赤唐辛子を中心に全部で7種類の香辛料を混ぜた粉末状の薬味。利用範囲は広い。

SHICHIMI TOGARASHI

A mixture of seven spices based around red pepper, it has a wide range of uses.

粉山椒

山椒の実を粉末にした薬味で、うなぎの蒲焼きや焼き鳥などに用いられます。

SANSHO (JAPANESE PEPPER)

This is powdered peppercorns from the Japanese pepper tree, and it is used to spice grilled eel, chicken, etc.

練りわさび

辛味とさわやかな香りがある日本原産のわさびを、練ってチューブに詰めたもの。

WASABI

Ground Japanese *wasabi* (horseradish) combines spicy taste with a refreshing aroma. It is available in a tube.

練り辛子

和辛子はマスタードと違い、ビネガーが入っていないので辛みが強い。

JAPANESE MUSTARD

Unlike Western mustard, ground Japanese *karashi* is not made with vinegar and is very hot.

青のり

海藻の一種である青のりを粉末状にしたもの。

AO-NORI (SEAWEED)

A type of seaweed. *Aonori* comes in powder form.

日本の調理道具

日本で一般に使われている便利な道具を紹介します。

Japanese Cooking Utensils

This section introduces the most commonly used cooking implements in a Japanese kitchen.

しゃもじ

ご飯を混ぜたり盛ったりするときに使う木製の杓子。金属製より木製のほうが、ご飯がつきにくい。水で濡らして使います。

WOODEN SPATULA

This wooden spatula is used for mixing or serving rice. Compared to metal products, it is less prone to stick. Wet the spatula before use.

菜箸

調理用の箸。竹製で食事用の箸より長く、長さによって大中小があります。

COOKING CHOPSTICKS

This cooking chopsticks are usually longer than ordinary bamboo chopsticks, and come in various sizes.

お玉杓子

金属製の杓子。汁物をすくうときに。

LADLE

A metal ladle used for serving soup.

おろし金

しょうがや大根などをすりおろすときに。上部に細かい目がついています。

GRATER

Used for grating ginger, *daikon*, etc. The lid has fine serrated holes.

みそこし器

みそを溶くときに、こし器にみそを入れてだし汁につけ、へらでこします。

***MISO* SIEVE**

This sieve is used to dissolve *miso* into soup. Place the *miso* in the sieve, dip in the *dashi* stock and dissolve the *miso* with a spatula.

すり鉢・すりこ木

すり鉢は陶製で、内面に刻み目が入っており、ごまや豆腐などを入れ、すりこ木ですりつぶします。長芋などをするときにも使います。

MORTAR AND PESTLE

The mortar and pestle are used to grind sesame, *tofu*, etc. The mortar has a rough surface. It is used to grind *nagaimo*, etc.

落としぶた

煮物をするとき、火の通り
をよくするため、材料の上
に直接のせます。なければ、
代わりにアルミホイルをの
せてもOK。

DROP LID

This is a lid that is placed
directly on to food while
it is cooking to increase
the heat. A piece of tinfoil
can be substituted in-
stead.

焼き網

魚や餅などをのせ、直火に
かけて使います。ほうろう
の網の上に金網がついてお
り、火が直接材料に当たら
ないようになっています。

GRILL RACK

This grill rack is used to
grill fish, rice cakes, etc.,
over a flame. It is made
so that the wire netting
will not come into direct
contact with the flame.

巻きす

細く割った竹を糸で編み連
ねたもの。巻き寿司を巻い
たり、厚焼き卵を成形する
ときなどに使います。

SUSHI MAT

A mat made from thin
strips of bamboo sewn
together. It is used to roll
sushi rolls, egg rolls, etc.

盤台

すし飯を作るときに使う木
製の桶。木はご飯がつきに
くく、水分を吸収するとい
う利点があります。

VAT

A wooden container used
for *sushi* rice. Rice does
not stick to wood, and in
addition, the wood ab-
sorbs water.

布巾

薄い麻と木綿の混合布。キ
ッチンペーパーのように調
理にも使います。

CHEESE CLOTH

Cloth made from cotton
and hemp. It is used in
the same way as kitchen
paper.

竹串

焼き鳥などの料理に用いる
ほか、材料の火の通り具合
を調べるときにも使います。

BAMBOO SKEWER

These bamboo skewers
are used for *yakitori* (grilled chicken) and also for
checking the condition of
the interior of foods while
they are cooking.

日本の器

和食器は色、形、素材などのバリエーションが豊富ですが、まず日常的なものから気軽に使ってみましょう。

Japanese Dishes

Japanese tableware comes in a wide variety of shapes, colors and materials. Here are some of the most common dishes in everyday use.

和食器の基本３点セットといえば、汁椀、飯椀、箸です。この３点は、家庭では各自、自分用が決まっているのが普通です。汁椀は持ったときに熱くないよう木製で、漆器もありますが、これは高級品なのであまり日常使いはしません。

おかず用の器は、平皿、鉢、小皿があれば、たいがい事足ります。平皿は焼き物や炒め物などを盛る器で、長方形のものはよく魚料理に用いられます。丸皿もあります。

鉢は大きさや深さがいろいろあり、それによって煮物や和え物などを盛ったり、各自の取り分け皿にしたり、使い道はさまざま。小皿は、しょうゆや薬味などを入れるときに使います。ほかに、箸置きや湯飲みなどもあるといいでしょう。

家庭での箸は塗り箸が一般的ですが、お店では使い捨ての割り箸が使われます。割り箸も大衆品から高級品まで種類が多く、箸袋に趣向が凝らされたものもあります。

It is said that the three staples of Japanese tableware are a soup bowl, a rice bowl and a pair of chopsticks.

In most homes, everyone will have their own personal set of these items. The soup bowl is generally made of wood, so that it will not conduct heat when held. Sometimes it is made of lacquer ware, but since this is expensive it is not used for everyday meals.

Side dishes are served on flat plates, bowls, small plates, etc. Fried or grilled foods are served on flat plates, while fish are often served on rectangular plates. Round plates are also common.

Bowls come in various sizes and depths. They are used for dishes such as stews and cooked foods according to personal taste. Small dishes are used for soy sauce or condiments. Don't forget the chopstick rests and teacups too!

At home, most people will use painted chopsticks, but disposable chopsticks are common in restaurants. These disposable chopsticks vary in quality from coarse to smooth, and there is also great variety in the decorated chopstick envelopes.

奥は祝い用の箸袋に入った高級割り箸。
手前はごく普通の割り箸。

High-quality disposable chopsticks in a decorative for celebrations envelope (rear). Ordinary disposable chopsticks (front).

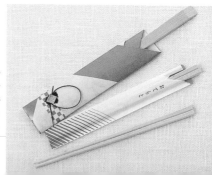

平皿
Flat plate

小鉢
Small bowl

湯飲み
Tea cup

飯椀
Rice bowl

箸置き
Chopstick rest

箸
Chopsticks

汁椀
Soup bowl

小皿
Small plate

＊箸は太いほうを右にして一番手前に置き、
その向こうに右に汁椀、左に飯椀を置くのが、配膳の決まりです。

＊Place the chopsticks nearest the table edge, with the
thick end to the right. As a rule, the soup bowl
goes on the right and the rice bowl on the left.

食事の作法

改まった席での作法は細かくいろいろありますが、ここでは基本的なことを取り上げます。

Dining Etiquette

There are many levels of etiquette depending on the occasion and the situation, but this section introduces advice on basic table manners that apply everywhere.

洋食のマナーでは、音をたててスープなどをすするのは絶対のタブーですが、和食の場合は気にしません。熱い汁物やお茶を飲むとき、麺類をすするときに音をたててかまいません。ざるそばは、音を立てて勢いよくするのが通ともいわれています。

湯飲みや杯は、女性の場合、右手で持って左手を添え、その状態で飲むのがマナーです。徳利でお酒を注ぐときも両手で持ちます。男性の場合は片手でかまいません。

In the West, it is thought impolite to make a slurping noise when sipping soup, etc., but in Japan there is no such taboo. You can make a noise when sipping hot liquids such as soup, tea and noodles. In fact, with *zarusoba*, it's thought polite to slurp the noodles forcefully and noisily.

With tea, it is good manners for women to lift the cup with the right hand and hold the bottom of the cup with the left. Women should also use both hands when pouring *sake* from the bottle into a cup. Men are allowed to use one hand.

箸のタブー
Chopstick taboos

握り箸
箸を持ったまま器を持つこと。器を持つときは、箸は食卓に置きます。

Nigiribashi
The act of holding the chopsticks while moving a bowl. When you move a bowl or plate, always put the chopsticks down on the table.

箸の持ち方
How to hold chopsticks

1. 右手で箸を取ります。

   Pick up the chopsticks with the right hand.

2. 左手を下から添えます。

   Hold with the left hand from below.

3. 右手を回し、箸を下から持ちます。

   Turn the right hand, and take the chopsticks from the bottom.

4. 1本を人差し指と中指の先で軽くはさんで親指の先を添え、もう1本は親指の根元と薬指で固定します。

   Place one chopstick lightly in between the index and middle fingers, and secure with the thumb. Place the other chopstick in between the thumb and third finger.

拾い箸
食べ物を箸から箸に渡すこと。火葬場で遺骨を渡すときの風習なので、もっとも嫌われる箸使いです。

Hiroibashi
Passing food from chopsticks to chopsticks. This action is greatly disliked because it is customary to handle ashes in this way at the crematorium.

寄せ箸
箸を使って器を寄せること。器は箸を置いて、手で持ち上げて取り寄せます。

Yosebashi
Using chopsticks to lift a bowl. Put the chopsticks down, and lift the bowl by hand to move it.

刺し箸
食べ物を箸で刺して食べること。必ず箸ではさんで食べます。

Sashibashi
Using the chopsticks to impale food. Chopsticks must always be used to grip food.

度量衡
Weights and Measures

● 容量
Quantity

小さじ 1 = 1 tsp =5ml
大さじ 1 = 1 Tbsp =15ml
1 カップ= 1 Japanese cup =200ml
1 U.S. cup =240〜250ml
1 ounce (fl oz)=30ml

※ml=cc

Milliliters	Spoons	Japanese cup	U.S. cup	Fluid Ounces
5ml	1 tsp			
15m	1 Tbsp			
50ml	3 Tbsp + 1 tsp	$\frac{1}{4}$ cup	$\frac{1}{5}$ cup	$1\frac{2}{3}$ oz
60ml	4 Tbsp		$\frac{1}{4}$ cup	2 oz
80ml	5 Tbsp + 1 tsp		$\frac{1}{3}$ cup	$2\frac{2}{3}$ oz
100ml	6 Tbsp + 2 tsp	$\frac{1}{2}$ cup	$\frac{2}{5}$ cup	$3\frac{1}{3}$ oz
120ml	8 Tbsp		$\frac{1}{2}$ cup	4 oz
150ml	10 Tbsp	$\frac{3}{4}$ cup	$\frac{3}{5}$ cup	5 oz
200ml	13 Tbsp + 1 tsp	1 cup	$\frac{4}{5}$ cup	$6\frac{2}{3}$ oz
240ml	16 Tbsp	$1\frac{1}{4}$ cup	1 cup	8 oz
400ml		2 cups	$1\frac{2}{3}$ cups	13 oz
600ml		3 cups	$2\frac{1}{2}$ cups	20 oz
800ml		4 cups	$3\frac{1}{3}$ cups	27 oz
1600ml		8 cups	$6\frac{2}{3}$ cups	53 oz

＊英文のレシピ内の数字は正確に換算したものではなく、
わかりやすいように、大まかな数字に直してあります。

＊All measurements in the English recipes
are rough approximations only.

●温度
Temperature

揚げ油の温度	Frying oil temperature
低温160〜165℃	low 320〜330°F
中温170〜175℃	medium 340〜350°F
高温175〜180℃	high 350〜360°F

●重量
Weight

grams ×0.035= ounces
ounces ×28.35= grams

Grams	Ounces	Pounds
10 g	$\frac{1}{3}$ oz	
15 g	$\frac{1}{2}$ oz	
20 g	$\frac{2}{3}$ oz	
30 g	1 oz	
40 g	$1\frac{2}{5}$ oz	
50 g	$1\frac{3}{4}$ oz	
60 g	2 oz	
85 g	3 oz	
100 g	$3\frac{1}{2}$ oz	
115 g	4 oz	$\frac{1}{4}$ lb
140 g	5 oz	
150 g	$5\frac{1}{4}$ oz	
170 g	6 oz	
200 g	7 oz	
225 g	8 oz	$\frac{1}{2}$ lb
300 g	$10\frac{1}{2}$ oz	
320 g	11 oz	
340 g	12 oz	$\frac{3}{4}$ lb
360 g	$12\frac{1}{2}$ oz	
400 g	14 oz	
450 g	16 oz	1 lb
500 g	18 oz	
570 g	20 oz	$1\frac{1}{4}$ lbs
600 g	21 oz	
800 g	28 oz	
900 g	$31\frac{1}{2}$ oz	2 lbs
1kg	35 oz	$2\frac{1}{4}$ lbs

●長さ
Length

cm ×0.39= inches
inch ×2.54= cm

Centimeters	Inches
5 cm	$\frac{1}{5}$ inch
1 cm	$\frac{2}{5}$ inch
1.5 cm	$\frac{1}{2}$ inch
2 cm	$\frac{4}{5}$ inch
2.5 cm	1 inch
3 cm	1.2 inches
4 cm	1.5 inches
5 cm	2 inches
6.5 cm	2.5 inches
8 cm	3 inches
10 cm	4 inches
15 cm	6 inches
20 cm	8 inches

料理製作・スタイリング Cooking・Styling
八巻めぐ実 Megumi Yamaki

撮影 Photographs
泉 健太 Kenta Izumi

翻訳 Translation
沢田美和子 Miwako Sawada

翻訳監修 Translation Supervision
リチャード・ジェフリー Richard Jeffery

デザイン Design
DOTinc.

構成 Direction
佐藤雅美 Masami Sato

編集 Editorial
池田書店 Ikeda Shoten Publishing Co., LTD.

英語訳つき
和食の基本
JAPANESE RECIPES 60

●協定により検印省略

編　者　株式会社池田書店
発行者　池田 豊
印刷所　図書印刷株式会社
製本所　図書印刷株式会社
発行所　株式会社池田書店
　　　　〒162-0851 東京都新宿区弁天町43番地
　　　　電話03-3267-6821（代）
　　　　振替00120-9-60072
＊落丁・乱丁はおとりかえいたします。

©IKEDASHOTEN 2004, Printed in Japan
ISBN4-262-12916-0